Taking Down the Wall

Taking Down the Wall

Christine Murphy

To order additional copies of this book, contact:
Xlibris Corporation
1-888-795-4274
www.Xlibris.com
Orders@Xlibris.com
53549

Contents

This book is dedicated
to all the people who
heard my story and said,
"You should write
a book!"

Acknowledgements

These acknowledgements go far beyond thanking people for their help with this book. I shamelessly use this opportunity to recognize the men, women and children who have supported and guided my life's journey.

Mom and Dad, there are not enough ways to say "thank you" for all you have provided. Not only have you been amazing as parents, but as parents-in-law and grandparents too. Generations to come will have a love of nature, a generous spirit and faith in God because of your models. Dad, thanks for teaching me how to fish! Mom, thanks for taking me to the Sugar Shack and for letting me stay up late to watch Johnny Carson (sis-boom-baa.)

Danny, my older and wiser brother, you changed my life with one simple word, "Okay." I am forever grateful.

Martha, you may be my little sister, but many times along this journey, you proved to be wise beyond your years. Thank you for helping me turn my story into a book. Thank you for marrying a really nice guy and for having kids, although you don't seem nearly old enough for either.

Murph, enjoy the motorcycle . . . you earned it. I don't know where I would be without you. Thank you for all the times you gave me space and especially for all the times you didn't.

Allison, I am so proud to be your Mom. You have grown into a wonderful person and I am grateful for your questions. So many times, I knew if I understood the situation enough to explain it to you, I must really get it myself.

Cole, thank you for all your care and support along the way. You are so grown up these days. Thank you for all the times that you started dinner and helped around the house without being asked. Thank you for being so willing to "go along for the ride."

Katie, you are an inspiration. I am in awe of your outlook on life, your loving attitude and especially your dance moves. Do me one favor and take it easy on the cats?

The other Murph, (my father-in-law), over these years I have come to count you among my closest friends. I am thankful for all the times you offered a shoulder to cry on and a listening ear. I wish Linda were here to see how it all unfolded.

Jenny, thank you for being so smart, so smart that you knew you couldn't tell me the answers; I would have to find them for myself. I am grateful to have found you.

Ray you are the ambassador of peace. I am grateful for your patience and your sense of humor. The combination of the two got us through many tough moments.

Richard, I thank you for the challenge. I hope that comes across as the compliment that it is meant to be. Things easily gained are not always appreciated. I do truly appreciate who you are and what you bring to my life.

Diane, it has been a long road for both of us. Thank you for having the courage to send me that birthday card. It led to changes in my life that reach far beyond our initial meeting.

Stacie, may God bless you for the amazing friend you have been to my family and me. I owe you for a million things but the top of the list would be for rum cake, a food that feeds the mind, body and soul.

Mary, you have truly changed my life. So many times, after our talks I felt ready to take big chances. I knew no matter the outcome, you would be there to congratulate me or comfort me, many times both.

Carolyn, how can I ever thank you for the wisdom and guidance you have provided, not just in these past two years. We met 10 years ago because I needed your help and a tremendous friendship resulted. You are a gift.

Rana, I am indebted to you for the many times you allowed me to pour out my soul. Your acceptance helped me to see myself as a better person and to come to terms with the true meaning of the word *past*.

Linda, thank you for providing balance. So many times when others were saying, "go, go, go" you helped me by saying, "I'm not sure about that." I am grateful for all the times you listened and supported my feelings.

Jackie, like many of the others on this list, we met because you were my child's teacher. How could I know that you would really end up teaching *me* so much more? I am thankful for your insight and your encouragement.

Bonnie, oh what I wouldn't give to have us live closer. Three hours away is just too far. You have been so much more than a friend. We go a long way back and I can't imagine where I would be without you. Thanks for the million times you cried with me and for the million times more that you made me laugh. Thank you for marrying a great guy and having beautiful girls. I love you all.

Linda, my parallel life twin, you have weaved in and out of my life for so many years. I won't lose touch with you ever again. You have sacrificed so much sleep for me; midnight phone calls rule!

Maureen, when I met you over four years ago, I could never imagine the impact you would have on my life. Thank you for reminding me to breathe.

Martha, Roy and Trish, my editors-at-large, thank you for the compliments and above all for the helpful suggestions. I appreciate the time and energy you each devoted to *my* project.

Chapter 1

HOW IT ALL STARTED

In June 2003, my mother-in-law was diagnosed with lung cancer. I purchased a journal, hoping she would document her thoughts and feelings. On the first page I wrote, "Sometimes the best stories come from an unexpected journey." She died a year later without having written one word. I took the book home and tucked it away in a drawer.

I have since filled those pages with my own unexpected journey. I am a person who shares my life, not much remains a secret. When significant events happen, I find myself telling the same story over and over again. In the summer of 2007, I told my story many times, and I always started it the same way, "It all started with a bad mammogram." I would go on to tell a story of transformation, a story of emotional and spiritual growth.

*   *   *

To understand the changes that took place, it is necessary to know some of my history. The story starts in the summer of 1968 when I was conceived. The man and the woman were not married; in fact, he was married to somebody else. The woman left town without telling anyone, not even the man she was pregnant. She stayed away from home and decided to place me for adoption. Her family found out about my impending arrival and her mother was present for the birth. About 10 days later, the woman signed the papers to relinquish me and then tried to go on with her life.

As for me, I left the hospital and lived with a foster family for a couple of months before meeting the people who would eventually become my parents. A letter arrived one day to tell my parents there was a girl available and they should make an appointment to meet me. They went in on a Monday, saw me, said, "Yes" and then returned on Friday to bring me home. Except we did not go home because it was Memorial Day weekend, we went camping. My father was setting up camp when some friends arrived. He told them they should go knock on the trailer door because my mother had something new to show them. They knocked and my mother opened the door allowing them to see me sleeping in a laundry basket. I now was part of a family. I had a mom, a dad, and an older brother. Danny was adopted two and a half years earlier.

I don't really remember being told I was adopted. It was just something I always knew. I talked about it here and there growing up. In school, kids would sometimes accuse me of lying when I said I was adopted. My brother was adopted as was a neighbor, so for us, it was not unusual. I think we found it amusing more than anything else. I could not help myself if someone said I looked just like my father. I would reply, "That's funny because I was adopted."

When I was just shy of seven, my mother told us she was pregnant. I can remember dancing around the living room thinking it would be cool to have a little brother or sister. I never gave it much thought that this child would be biological to my parents. As we got older, I always felt that fact added to the story. Here are these two people; they want nothing more than to have a family. They had no luck becoming parents "the old-fashioned way" so they adopt two children and live a lovely life. Then, when the mother is 39 and the father is 41, a baby girl is born. I am sure all the adults in our lives could appreciate what having that baby meant. I thought it was cool. Though I was quite the tomboy at that age, I wore a dress to the hospital when I met Martha because it seemed to be a special occasion like no other.

In the second grade, I won second prize in a writing contest. Each student in the class wrote an essay titled, "My Mother is Terrific Because . . ." In my essay, I wrote that I knew my mother loved me because I was adopted. My parents must have explained at one time or another I was chosen. I wrote that I felt special because "out of all those other babies, she picked me." I definitely had the vision in my head that my parents went into a room full of babies and said, "We'll take that one." For a little extra emphasis on how much she loved me, I also added she came to see me everyday in the hospital when I had my tonsils out.

* * *

Life went on pretty much as one might expect for the next few years. Dad worked and Mom stayed home. We went to church, visited family out of town, took vacations at the lake and ate dinner every night at 5:15. Mom was a den leader and a troop leader for scouts. She volunteered for PTA committees and took us to swim lessons at the YMCA. Dad taught us how to fish, water ski and drive the boat. We spent the last two weeks of every July at Schroon Lake, a truly special place to all of us.

I don't really know how often I thought about being adopted. It wasn't daily, weekly or monthly. It was just every once in a while. It was on Mother's Day and Father's Day, it was on my birthday, it was when I saw the movie *Annie* or any other movie that highlighted orphans or adoption.

When I was young, younger than 12 or so, I think all my thoughts about adoption were positive. In church school, the nun explained that God was everybody's father and the Virgin Mary was everybody's mother. I told a classmate how lucky I was because it meant that I had three mothers and three fathers. I felt like I had a leg up on the rest of the kids.

Around 12 or 13 is when there were a few bumps in the road. Being a new teenager had its difficulties, and I started to think about the people who made me, and then did not keep me. A very *basic* understanding of how babies were made probably accounted for this curiosity. Just about every book or after school special talked about the subject in the same manner. "When a mommy and a daddy love each other very much, they decide to make a baby." At that age, I don't think I understood that people had sex for reasons other than making babies. I don't recall there being any specials that talked about what happens when the mommy and daddy are not married, the pregnancy is unplanned, and they are not ready to take care of the baby.

I can remember talking to a neighbor. I was curious about my adoption and what my biological parents might be like. She encouraged me to talk to my mother; she was sure it would be okay. I remember it as if it were yesterday. My mother was washing the windows in the dining room; her back was to me. As she reached up high to clear a streak I said, "Mom, what do you know about my biological mother?" Without turning around, she said the woman was a nurse, about 21-years-old and not married. She said the father was probably a doctor; maybe it was a supply room romance. (My parents were not given any information about the father. This was Mom's best guess.) She made it sound romantic. I suppose my difficulty with this was trying to reconcile, if it was so lovely, then why didn't they keep me.

When I was 14 or 15 years old, my Girl Scout leader had a baby girl. I can picture myself sitting on the edge of the bed holding her. She was a few weeks old. Two friends were with me when I said, "How could anyone throw one of these away?" (I did not have feelings like this often.) My views on getting pregnant were so skewed. My parents were married for 17 years before my sister came along. It just did not seem to be an easy process. On the other hand, a girl one grade ahead of me was having her second baby as a junior in high school. That girl kept her babies though. It was confusing to think something that had been so difficult for my parents, happened so easily for others. I really started to wonder what kind of person gave away her baby. In retrospect I can see how immature I was and how I had no idea that sometimes, things just happen.

Throughout high school and college when I spoke of being adopted, people would frequently ask if I had interest in finding my biological parents. Over the years my answer never changed, a definitive, "No." On a scale of one to 10, I felt a person's curiosity would have to rank at least a 9.5 to do a search. My interest measured somewhere around a 0.6.

*   *   *

As a kid, my brother Danny was tall and skinny. Mom used to compare him to the handle on the vacuum cleaner. He had dark brown eyes like our mother and his skin tanned during the summer. I was covered with freckles. He had an adventurous spirit and he always found a way to make vehicles go higher and faster. I learned slang from my brother and can still hear his young voice saying, "De-cent" when a cool car or truck passed us on the road.

I can only remember talking with my brother about being adopted one time. He was having struggles, difficulty in school, smoking, drinking and lots of arguing with everyone. We were camping and there was some kind of disagreement with our parents. I looked at him and said, "Don't you ever think of how lucky we are? How we could have ended up with other families?" He looked at me and said, "I don't want to talk about it," so we didn't.

My brother's difficulties escalated and he ran away several times. He entered a teen drinking program more than once. He quit school and moved out of the house. At the time, I could not understand any of it. We stopped going on the yearly vacations, dinner was not always at 5:15 anymore and "stress" became part of my vocabulary at far too young an age. I certainly felt he was ruining the family. An unbelievable anger developed toward him. I eventually stopped talking to him and made it clear I did not even want to be around him. If he walked in a room, I walked out.

While my brother was struggling, I worked overtime to prove I was not like him. The drive to succeed was fueled when a teacher in the high school stopped me one day early in my freshman year. He wanted to know, "So are you going to be like your brother?" I knew what he was trying to imply. Danny cut school and started each school day in the smoking area. Trying to establish my own identity, I did well in school, played an instrument, competed in sports and earned my Gold Award in Girl Scouts. I was a popular babysitter, the editor of my high school yearbook and the MVP of my field hockey team, an all-around over achiever.

*   *   *

I knew at a young age I wanted to work with young children, special needs children. I set my sights on being a speech language pathologist. I was accepted to a college with a great speech department. On Labor Day, my parents dropped me off and I finally had what I wanted. I was in control of my own life, making my own decisions. Then the rug slipped out from under me. I found myself in unfamiliar territory. In high school, I could make good grades without studying. In college, you actually have to study! Why didn't somebody tell me? Why didn't somebody warn me skipping classes was not a good idea? Why didn't somebody tell me playing cards into the wee hours of the morning on a weeknight would probably cause me to oversleep and miss my 8 a.m. class? In all fairness, somebody did try to tell me all these things. The problem was it was my mother, but since she had not been to college, I did not consider her a reliable source.

I failed out of my freshman year, not once, but twice. When the fall semester grades arrived, I had failed out but there was a process for appeal. I went back to my high school to ask three teachers for letters of recommendation. I had been in the top 10 percent of the class at one point and was in the honor society. Now I had to try to explain what had happened. A tough feat since I really did not know myself. With letters in hand, I went out to school, telling a room full of deans I had seen the errors of my ways and I would not make the same mistakes twice. They agreed to let me come back for the spring semester on academic probation. I did work harder, and my grades did improve, but only slightly. Opening my spring grades was a tough day. I had failed out again. I was embarrassed. I had let my family down. I moved home, got a job and enrolled in community college. I told my parents I would pay for everything my sophomore year, tuition, books and gas for the car. I would not expect them to pay for my mistake.

I got my act together, made very good grades and then applied to a different four-year school to continue studies for speech pathology. I was accepted and ready to go for the fall semester in August 1989. As the saying goes, if you want to hear God laugh, tell him your plans. I had my plan. Go back to college, get my degree, and go on with my life.

*   *   *

At the end of July, I was babysitting for some friends at their lake house when I heard eight important words: "Murph, this is Crissy. Crissy, this is Murph." I was immediately drawn to his teddy bear-qualities, big, cuddly and furry (a beard and a moustache). There was warmth about him physically and emotionally. Three very unofficial dates and six days later, I told my friend Mary Beth I was going to marry Murph. She warned, "I don't know if he is looking for a wife." To which I replied, "He better be."

I left for school at the end of August. Four months later, we were engaged. The following year I graduated with my bachelor's degree in May and then we got married in June. We moved to Plattsburgh, two hours away from our hometown so I could start graduate school in July.

Shortly after earning my master's degree, we moved back closer to our families, and I was hired at a local special needs preschool. Life was going all according to the plan. Then, God laughed.

Chapter 2

BLIND-SIDED

It was an ordinary Thursday night. Murph and I were eating dinner and watching television. The phone rang. I went to the kitchen to answer it.

"Hello."

"Is this Christine Murphy?"

"Yes?"

"Did you used to be Christine Warmus?"

"Who is this?"

"Were you born on March 5th 1969?"

"Who is this?" I said in a stern voice.

"My name is Diane and I had a baby on March 5th 1969. I placed her for adoption and I think you are my baby."

From that moment, things get just a bit fuzzy in my memory. I do remember screaming in a way I had never done before. I remember trying to grab on to the small table because I thought I would pass out. I remember my husband running in. I tried to tell him through my shrieks, "The person on the other end thinks she is my biological mother." He picked the phone up from the floor. To this day, I don't know why he didn't just hang up. It was a surreal moment. Later Murph would tell me, he was certain from my intense reaction, that my parents had been killed in an accident. It was the only thing he could think of that would cause me to react that way.

He spoke with her for a moment, took down her phone number and then hung up. I was sitting in a chair at this point but could still feel the table shaking in front of me as I tried to steady myself. Murph hugged me and tried to calm me down.

I called my parents immediately. We only lived twenty minutes away, but I didn't think I could wait that long to tell them. My mother answered the phone and I asked her to get my dad on the extension. When they were both on the phone, I burst into tears saying I had just received a call from someone who thinks she is my biological mother. I was hysterical and needed to hand the phone to Murph. Luckily, everyone else was a little more level headed than I was. My father suggested we call back and ask a few questions to be sure it was the right person. My adoption file was sealed. We had no idea of the birthmother's name.

My husband called back and said he wanted to ask a few questions. He asked how old she was now and how old she was at the time of the birth. He asked what she was doing at the time of the birth. He asked what medical information was provided at the time of the adoption. My mother had previously told me the birthmother was 21 at the time, a nurse and had many allergies. When my husband asked the questions, she said she was 21, in nursing school and had many allergies. It seemed like a match. It seemed like a nightmare. How on earth did she find me? Why did she find me? What did she want from me?

Murph eventually asked if I wanted to speak with my birthmother. I had a brief conversation with her; I don't remember much of it. She told me she had two sons, my birthfather had passed away and he had other children too. All of it was confusing. She provided some information on how she found me. Something about DMV records and birthdates and lots of phone calls. She said bits and pieces about medical information. She talked about *always* wanting to find me. She talked about details, the time I was born and how much I weighed. She told me she named me Rebecca. The only thing I can remember saying was, "Thank you for not having an abortion." We hung up once again.

I called a couple of friends from high school and college. I would open with, "In all the years you have known me, did I ever say I wanted to find my biological mother?" I felt like I needed to confirm what my position had been on the subject. The person on the other end would say, "No, why?" I repeated what had just happened. Each would ask what I was going to do and I didn't have a clue.

Murph went to bed and suggested I try to get some sleep. Not much luck there. Around midnight, I felt compelled to call my birthmother a second time. She told me a bit more about her sons, how old they were and what they were doing in life. She gave me the name of my birthfather. She told me he was a farmer and their relationship had been brief. She said she did not tell anyone she was pregnant and left town to go to nursing school. I was so unsure of everything, I did not know if I wanted to keep talking or if I wanted to hang up. After 15 or 20 minutes, I ended the call. We had exchanged addresses and I had agreed to send a letter.

*   *   *

The next morning, after Murph left for work I called Dawn. She was a friend as well as my former teacher in high school. I told her of the call from the night before. Her next statement took me by surprise.

"Now I can finally tell you."

"Tell me what?" I asked.

"I can tell you a year ago, I was contacted by the dean of the high school. The dean said someone from Social Services had contacted her, asking about you, and if she knew if you wanted to be found."

"What did you say?"

"In all the time I've known you, you never once expressed a desire to look or be found."

"When exactly did this happen?"

"Three weeks before your wedding."

I drove up to my parents' house. I told them again of the call from my birthmother and the information she provided to me. My mother nonchalantly said, "Let's have her over for dinner." I promptly went to the bathroom and threw up. How could she possibly suggest that? Never the two worlds shall meet was my only thought.

My father and I went out in the backyard. We sat in lawn chairs as if we were about to casually discuss the weather. He told me he and my mother loved me, and that I was an adult and I could do whatever I wanted to do, and it was okay if I wanted to meet her and nobody could ever take me from them. He used his "father-voice" as he spoke. I don't think I believe in reincarnation, but if I did, I think my father must have been a great philosopher is a previous life. When he used this particular tone of voice, everything he said seemed to make perfect, rational sense.

I asked him to go to the Social Services Department with me to find out more. We went down and spoke to a caseworker. She informed me I could get the non-identifying information out of my file by filling out a request. She gave me the number for the New York State Adoption Registry. If my birthmother were also registered, I would be given her identifying information.

Throughout the next couple of days, I told people I was living a "Movie of the Week" scenario, and I wondered when Oprah was going to be showing up at my door.

I also got in touch with the dean of students who took the mystery call from social services the year before. I told the dean the name of the worker I met with the day before. I was amazed when she said it was the same person who called her. The dean said the worker indicated my birthmother was attempting to get the file opened because of medical information. I was infuriated and wanted to go to the caseworker's boss and demand she be fired. How dare she open my confidential file!

I confronted this worker a day later and, at first, she denied it. Then when I provided details, the name of the person she called and what was discussed; she admitted she made the call. She assured me she never gave out my name and did not know how my birthmother found me. She ended by saying my birthmother seemed desperate to find me.

*   *   *

My birthmother and I exchanged letters. The one she wrote to me was lengthy and included lots of information on extended family. There were photos. One picture was of her and her sons, on the back she wrote, "This is us. Your other family." It was overwhelming. I sent a letter with very little information. I made it clear in the letter that I never wanted to be found and frankly, I was in shock. I shared that I had a brother and a sister. I told her that my life was good and that I was happy. I did send a couple photos. I do not know why, but I sent one of my wedding pictures.

I could not bring myself to call my birthmother by her name. Conversation involved references to "she" and "her." When I spoke of her and her sons, I used "the north country people," as they lived a couple hours north of us. She called a couple times. It was unnerving. I got edgy every time the phone rang. I didn't feel like I had anything to say to her. I finally asked one day that she not call anymore. Perhaps letters would be the better way to communicate.

I continued to talk to friends and family about the situation. I was always hoping somebody would say, "Here's what you should do . . ." and then fill in the blank with something that felt right. Unfortunately, many people suggested I meet her; not a comfortable thought.

After the initial talks with my parents, they did not ask much. I think they saw how upset the whole thing made me and felt it was best to let time take its course. I found it interesting they did not talk about it either. When I would see friends, neighbors and relatives, they had no idea what was going on. If it was no big deal, why weren't they telling the story?

*   *   *

I started my new job in September at a special needs preschool. It felt good to have something to concentrate on other than the adoption situation. It didn't take long though for me to start asking my new co-workers for their opinions. One day I brought photos of the north country people into work. I asked a few people if they thought I resembled the people in the pictures. Interestingly enough, two other people on the very small staff were also adopted. It was settling to talk to others who could maybe understand how I felt. Neither of them ever wanted to search and both commented they would feel similarly to me had they received that call.

A few weeks into the job, I asked to speak with our school psychologist and told him about the call from my birthmother. He recommended someone for me to see and I promptly made an appointment. I don't remember the psychologist's name. What I do remember is that he asked me if I wanted to meet my birthmother, and I said no. Then he said, "So don't."

"But she *is* the person who gave birth to me."

He told me it did not mean I *owed* her anything. I liked this guy. He gave me the answer I was looking for, but still I was hesitant. Could it be that easy? Just don't do it? I said, "But what if it was the other way around? What if I had done the searching and then when I found her she wouldn't see me?"

He asked a few questions about my family and my relationships. After our brief discussion, he quickly noticed the not-so-practical "care taker" role I regularly assumed. When he questioned me about it, all I could say was, "You should meet my mother." I emulated my mother in many ways, not all of them were healthy. After two appointments, I stopped seeing the psychologist.

By the end of October, I realized I did not want the reunion situation to continue. I contemplated for a long time how to convey my feelings to my birthmother. I didn't think I could do it on the phone. After much reflection and lots of input from friends, I wrote my birthmother a letter. I wrote that I had given it a lot of thought and I felt this just was not the time in my life for this to happen. Perhaps in five years I would feel differently, perhaps not. I realized my decision would be hard for her but I needed to do what was best for me. I asked she only contact me should she have a change of address and noted I would do the same. I wrote the letter and tried to wait a couple weeks before mailing it. I wanted to be sure of my feelings. I only made it to day three before I addressed the envelope and sent it on its way.

For a few weeks I held my breath to see if she would respond. She did not.

*   *   *

Three months after I ended contact with my birthmother, the phone rang and it was her younger son. His voice was stern and confrontational. He wanted to know why I would not meet her. The heated exchange lasted about 10 minutes and ended with me yelling into the phone, "Don't ever call me again, I already have a family and you are not it!" The next morning, I changed our phone number and had it unlisted. I became a little paranoid after that. On the phone, the son mentioned his mother had contacted a private investigator during her search for me. I began to feel like I was being followed. I did not like being home alone, and I never wanted to answer the door.

Our lives moved along over the next few years. We bought a house and I became pregnant with our first child. About the time of my baby shower, I received a certified package in the mail from my birthmother. I flipped out. In a panic, I called my husband, "There is a certified package at the post office and it is from my birthmother! What do you think it is? What if it is a baby present? What if she has seen me and knows that I am pregnant? What if she drives by our house all the time?" Very rationally, he answered, "I'll pick it up on the weekend, don't worry about it now." Did he know to whom he was talking? Not worry?

An hour later, I went to the post office myself. Nervously I signed for the package, went out to my car and opened it. Inside was a blue glass bell, a short note and an obituary. Her mother, my biological grandmother, had passed away and the bell was a gift from her. I looked at it for while and then tucked it away in the closet along with the letters I had received over the years.

People often asked if I thought more about my adoption when I was pregnant myself. I can't say that I did. What I did do, was look for physical similarities after my daughter was born. I did look a little like my mom (short in stature) and my dad (light eyes and a round face) but I always laughed it off. I suppose I was excited to see, for the very first time in my life, a person who was biologically related to me. I was 26 years old. My baby, however, looked exactly like her father, milk-white skin, light blue eyes and Irish-red hair. Every time somebody noted the likeness, I felt slighted. Baby number two arrived 17 months later and looked even *more* like his father. My son had all the same physical traits as my daughter but also had my husband's dimpled chin. I did not realize it at the time, but can see in retrospect that I did wish to see someone who looked like me. I had them at my disposal, three people anxiously waiting to meet me. I still could not do it.

*   *   *

In the spring of 1999, I was watching a show on adoption reunions. I noticed I did not have the usual pit in my stomach. At the end of the show, I went to get something outside. Standing there in the middle of my garage, God spoke to me. What I heard was not so much words, but a thought that was suddenly and inexplicably in my head, "Open the door." I took it to mean I was supposed to write a letter to my birthmother.

A day later, I went to talk to my mother. I started to cry and asked if God ever speaks to her. She asked what was going on. I explained how I thought God told me to write to my birthmother. She told me to do what I thought was right.

I did write a letter to my birthmother. I told her how I felt God wanted me to write to her. I told her that I didn't know what it all meant or where it would lead. In this letter, my birthmother learned for the first time, that I had given birth to two children. They were 4 and 2 at the time. I told her a little about the kids and included a few photos of my expanded family. I nervously waited for her reply, which arrived about a week later. She was glad to hear from me, glad to hear about the kids and glad my life was going well.

We exchanged another set of letters, but this time, when her letter arrived, the familiar pit was in my stomach again. There was a great deal of discussion of the past. She wrote about placing me for adoption and about her feelings. It was all too much and nothing I wanted to hear. I did not write back.

A couple months later, I found out I was pregnant for our third child. As I look at the timing of God's message and the letters, I truly feel God was trying to help me feel comfortable with the pregnancy. I was so secretive about the first two, not announcing their births in the paper. I knew my birthmother would think of my kids as her grandchildren. I feared her desire to know me, and them, would increase her obsession.

When my second daughter was born, she did resemble me, at least more than her brother or sister did. On sight of her red hair though, most people joked, "Will you try for another to get one that looks like you?" I sent my birthmother a letter about nine months later telling her about the baby. My notes to her tended to be casual, mostly in the present, not talking of my childhood or my feeling about adoption. I never offered to meet or resume phone calls.

*   *   *

Sometimes it was difficult because I did not know anyone who was in my same boat. I knew other adoptees but none had been found by the birth family. Luckily, I talked about it enough and my friends would tell me about stories they heard or people they knew. I refer to Carolyn as my sage friend. She is a speech pathologist, which automatically makes her smarter than most folks. She is a generation or so older than me and I value her life experience greatly. One day Carolyn told me she heard of a book (on Oprah) describing a scenario similar to mine. The author of *Ithaka*, Sarah, had her phone ring one day too. I immediately bought the book and read it with great interest. I was amazed to hear someone echo my feelings of uncertainty and confusion.

Time passed and I would occasionally receive a note or package from my birthmother. In August of 2002, 10 years after the initial contact, she sent me a hand-made quilt with a photo of her working on it. I did not know what to do with it. I offered it to my sister for a church bazaar but she would not take it. She told me to put it in the attic but *do not* get rid of it. Another time my birthmother sent an 8x10 framed photograph of herself. Into the closet it went with the letters, the glass bell and the quilt.

*   *   *

As a young girl in school, the nurse was taking my medical history for a sport physical. I told her how my mother's mother and brother had died at young ages from heart attacks and strokes. At the time, it did not occur to me that my mother and father's medical histories had no impact on mine.

Now that I was older and a mother myself, I did begin to wonder what I had genetically passed down. One thing mentioned in previous letters was a history of breast cancer. Both my biological grandmother and great-grandmother were diagnosed and eventually passed away. My doctor said that since I had a questionable history, I should start having mammograms at 35 instead of 40. Easy enough, right? I did indeed have my first mammogram at the age of 35. Two days later, I received a call. The woman from the clinic told me, "We would like another picture of your left breast." If I had a dime for every time I heard that! I had the follow up picture and all went well. Each year I had the mammogram and each year they called back for another picture, it was what I had come to expect.

In January 2007, I went in for my annual mammogram. Two days later, the phone rang. I expected the usual "we need another picture" comment. The woman on the other end said, "We need you to come back in to clear something we saw on your mammogram. We'd like you to have an ultrasound." None of that sounded good. She asked when I wanted to come in as if I were making an appointment for a pedicure. I told her I could be there in 10 minutes. Unfortunately, the next available appointment was an agonizing four hours later.

I called my husband and my sister to tell them about the call. My husband asked if I wanted him to meet me. I did want him there; I didn't know what they were going to do or say. He met me at two o'clock. They called me in, a technician and her student did the ultrasound. They began to talk to each other as if I were not there, talking about the size and location of "it." Two little letters, one small word. "It" had become the most important thing in my life.

The women completed their pictures and went to talk to the radiologist. They said they would be gone for about five minutes. As soon as the door closed, I started to cry. I had seen the screen. I had seen the "it." I had seen there was something there that did not look like it belonged. I was scared. At that point, my husband did the absolute best thing he could have. He did not say a word. He just held my hand and stroked my hair.

The technician came back in, "The radiologist felt it was a cyst and you should have it checked again in six months."

"What?"

"It is probably a cyst and cysts are typically benign."

"What?"

"You should follow up with you regular doctor and go over the results with her."

"If you were me, what would *you* do?" I asked the technician.

"Follow up with your doctor and get rechecked in six months."

I got dressed and we walked out to the parking lot. I knew we were outside and there was traffic and noise but at the same time, it was as if we were in a bubble. I looked at Murph.

"I want a second opinion."

"Okay."

"I want to be aggressive."

"Okay."

"Don't let anybody talk me out of it. Don't let anyone tell me to wait."

"Okay."

By this time, Murph was hugging me and the rest of the world came back into focus. I could hear the sounds of traffic and see cars driving along.

I called and made an appointment with my midwives' office. I went in and she reviewed the results of the ultrasound. I said I was nervous because I did not have a very clear family history. I wanted a second opinion. I wanted to be aggressive. I told her I didn't want to be a story in some magazine about waiting six months for a recheck and then finding out too late. She told me she agreed and I should see the surgeon before getting a second ultrasound.

About 10 days later, my husband and I were in the surgeon's office. He reviewed the information, did an exam and then spoke about his findings. He agreed with the radiologist it was probably a cyst. I looked at him and asked, "You can tell me 100 percent there is no cancer?" He said, "No, not 100 percent." I calmly stated, "Then take it out." Surgery was scheduled for three days later. I was not going to bet my health on *probably* and *typically*.

So, this was the beginning of my transformation. This was the beginning of my unexpected journey, and *it all started with a bad mammogram.*

*   *   *

I called my father-in-law to tell him about the surgery. He cried on the phone with me. I assured him I was not concerned, we were just being overly cautious, and I was feeling fine. I had to wonder if I would be penalized in heaven for the lies I had just told. I was indeed very concerned. My children were 11, 10 and 7. There was no way not to be concerned.

I talked to my parents. I burst into tears trying to tell them. My mother went straight for the "I'm sure it's nothing" routine. My dad talked about one of his sisters having a similar procedure a few years back. (This aunt died of cancer in 2001). My mother continued to reassure me all would be okay. Dad kept talking about his sister. My mother finally told him she didn't think using Aunt Vee as an example was a good idea. It did make me laugh though. Only my father would try to reassure my fears with the story of someone who died. I am sure my mother was frightened. However, I know her, and her mode is to make everything seem okay. I know it is because she cannot allow herself to get that scared about things. I am confident she prayed for me nonstop.

The day before the surgery, I cancelled my work visits for the next day, arranged for my sister to pick up the kids after school, talked to a few friends and mostly tried to stay calm. I did fairly well until about 9:30 that night. The kids were in bed and Murph and I were sitting on the couch watching television. Tears started to roll down one cheek and then the other. Soon the sniffling started. Murph put his hand on my knee and said, "I've been waiting for this to happen." He told me how much he loved me, he was there for me and we would handle things one step at a time. I was so grateful he did not try to tell me it was nothing and I shouldn't worry. I was scared and I needed him to be scared too.

I went to the hospital for the outpatient procedure in the morning. First, they inserted a guide wire into my breast to assist the surgeon in getting all the necessary tissue. Once they put the wire in, I was not allowed to move. A few *hours* later when my name was called, my husband and my father each leaned down to hug me. I wanted to grab onto them with all my might but I was not supposed to move. I did the best I could and gripped their hands, squeezing as hard as I could. Then the nurse wheeled me away on the gurney. The next thing I knew, it was finished. I was being told to take deep breaths. My husband, my father and now my father-in-law were around my bed. Once I was awake enough, my dad left to go home and reassure my mom that I was okay. My husband went out to get something from the car. I think he needed a few minutes alone to collect himself. So there I was, a little out of it from the anesthesia, talking to my father-in-law about having a piece of my breast removed. He just kept offering me sips of water through a straw.

The scar was bigger than I thought it would be. I was not prepared for how I would feel looking at it. While at the hospital, the woman in the bed next to me was having a mastectomy. I knew I should feel blessed I only had a chunk removed, not the whole breast. I was tired over the next week. The anesthesia affected me more than I thought. I kept reassuring my daughter Allison that I was okay but she didn't believe me. She confided that seeing me nap so frequently had her concerned.

I called the surgeon's office five days after the surgery to see if they had my results. Not yet. I called back two days later. Not yet. I resigned myself that I would find out when I found out and did not call again. I went to my follow up appointment 12 days after the surgery. The surgeon started to talk to me about the incision and asked if there was any pain. He eventually said, "You know your results, right?" I said, "No," holding my breath. He told me everything was fine; it was a cyst, no malignancy. I went out to the car and cried. Happy tears. I called my sister, my parents and two friends. I then pulled myself together and went to work as if it were any other day. A few days later, I was cleaning papers off the kitchen table when I found an unfinished note from my husband. He had written he was so glad I was okay. He wrote of how scared he was and how he had let himself start thinking about the "what-ifs." He also wrote how much he loved me. I took the note, turned it over and wrote, "I love you too!" I stuffed it inside his work boot.

Over those few weeks, I found a new appreciation for life. It sounds so clichéd but it is the truth. In particular, I found a new appreciation and a deeper love for my husband. He was everything I could have asked for and more. He took care of me, took care of the kids and took care of the house. We were on cloud nine. Life was all-good. I vowed that I would take nothing for granted. I would appreciate everything and everyone. I was settled with my plan. God was laughing once again.

Chapter 3

FACING MY FEARS

By the end of February, I was feeling back to my old self. Strike that. I was feeling better than my old self. One day I came home from work and stepped out of the car to check the mail. Two or three envelopes down, I saw a handwritten return address. I immediately recognized the penmanship. It was from my birthmother. I had not heard anything from her in about five years. Sitting back in the car, with my heart racing, I opened the envelope. It was a birthday card. Within one minute, I was on the phone with my sister telling her about the card. I was not happy with my birthmother. Why doesn't she leave me alone? What does she want from me? Why is she *always* bugging me?

My sister, being the rational person she is, asked me to read the card to her. It was a birthday card. On the inside, she wrote she hoped I was well (the nerve), the family was well (outrageous) and I would have a good birthday (how dare she). She said she would enjoy hearing from me again (don't hold your breath). My sister asked how long it had been since I had heard from her. I replied, "Five years." She commented it seemed my birthmother was trying to respect my position, she was just wishing me well and there did not seem to be too much pressure to respond. I quickly got off the phone with Martha, as she was clearly not on my side. I was looking for someone to echo my feelings. That turned out to be harder than I thought it would be.

I talked to a few friends. Most replied I should do what makes me comfortable. I just didn't know what that would be. My friend Linda is one of the people I turn to when I need a straightforward answer. She is usually more practical in her thinking; she encouraged me to take it slow.

*   *   *

About nine months earlier, I met Jenny, a psychotherapist who was helping my friend. I gave Jenny a call and asked if I could come in to discuss a situation. Luckily, she had an opening later in the day. I took it as a good sign and went in figuring she would hear my story and say, "Wow that is the most amazing thing I have ever heard. Yes, I would agree, she had no right to barge into your life and the nerve of her sending you a birthday card. I think you have handled it beautifully and would tell you to continue along the same course." Not so much.

Jenny sat in her chair and listened to my 35-minute rant. I told her I always knew I was adopted and it was no big deal. I told her about not wanting to search. I told her about the phone call from 15 years earlier. I told her about the first psychologist, how he told me I did not *owe* my birthmother anything. I told her about my mother wanting to have my birthmother over for dinner and how the very thought caused me to throw up. I told her about the letters. In fact, I had all the letters with me, and I pointed to them several times. I made the point of saying I gathered them from various places in the house. I certainly did not want to give the impression they were special or important. I didn't keep them all in one spot or anything. I told her about God speaking to me eight years earlier and how I wrote the letter but how the pit came back into my stomach a few weeks later. I told her how it was not fair and I didn't like it. Picture a 3-year-old being instructed to eat her spinach.

When I finished, Jenny took a deep breath and said; "I think you have some anger about your adoption."

"No, no, no, it is not about being *adopted*. I am fine with being *adopted*. It is about being *found*. It was a closed adoption. She was *never* supposed to find me."

It is funny how you can say one thing aloud, and have a completely different thought running through your head. While I "rationally" responded to her comment, my real feelings were quite the opposite. Is she even listening to me? How could she *possibly* think I am angry about the adoption?

"I think there *is* something about the adoption bothering you. You used words like devastating and traumatic when you described the initial phone call. If there weren't something about the adoption upsetting you, you probably would have been okay with being found. Many people in the same situation would probably welcome the contact," she explained.

I was not too happy with her take on it, but about 30 seconds later I had a thought: shit, she is right.

She went on to say, "Figuring things out does not mean you have to form a *relationship*. Even if you were to meet at some point, it may not develop into a significant *relationship*. Your *relationship* with your birthmother may begin at one point and then change over time."

My stomach churned. Is it warm in here or just me? "Could you stop saying *relationship*, because I think I am going to be sick?"

*   *   *

I went home feeling confused. Had I misjudged everything for all these years? Of all the things I hate in life, being wrong ranks near the top, probably right below mayonnaise. I spent time reading the old letters. I went to the library and checked out a few books on adoption and adoption reunions. I read the first book cover to cover in about two hours. I skipped the chapter on birthfathers since mine does not play a role in the current drama. I was intrigued by what I was reading. I had several "aha moments" as I read things which struck a chord with me. I also had several "that is a load of crap moments" as I read things I did not like.

I read late into the night and had trouble falling asleep. I turned on the television in our room hoping to drift off. I stopped changing channels to watch a rerun of a sitcom. The episode was about one of the characters being found by a child she had placed for adoption 20-odd years earlier. Coincidence?

The next day I began reading a book focused on adoptees and the idea that many of their issues come from having a broken inner child. I read about three pages of the book and placed it into the "load of crap" category. There was *nothing* broken about me. I tossed the book on my bedroom floor. Not good enough, I put it in the living room. It still bothered me so I put it in the car. I only felt relieved when I put that awful book in the return slot at that library. Good riddance!

I became frustrated with most of the books because rarely was my situation represented. Almost all the stories were of children searching out birthparents. Nearly every one of the stories reflected a positive outcome. Everyone involved became "whole" again. I do not question these situations happened and I don't mean to belittle those people's feelings. However, just for the record, I felt perfectly whole just as I was, thank you very much.

*   *   *

I continued my appointments with Jenny. They were difficult. I did not like asking for help. I constantly talked about how out of control I felt. Repeatedly, I talked about always being in control of myself, of situations. *I* was the person other people called when *they* needed help. I usually knew the answers. I questioned why I was even delving into this situation. I was living a happy life, why, after all these years should I revisit this difficult circumstance. Something beyond my control seemed to be the driving force. Even though the sessions were hard and exhausting, I kept calling the scheduler for my next appointment.

I talked with Jenny about growing up Catholic and being told premarital sex was a sin. It was not just premarital sex that brought about my life; it was adultery. For God's sake, that was on the top 10 list of things NOT to do. It was difficult to process my very existence was due to a sinful act. What did that make me?

Shortly after that conversation, the gospel reading at church was about Jesus and the woman accused of adultery. I listened with renewed interest to a verse I heard countless times before. "He who is without sin among you, let him throw the first stone at her." Hearing this verse was an awakening. God was aware of my confusion and He was trying to guide me. Each step forward also caused me to look back. I was certainly not without sin in my life. Who was I to judge my birthmother's actions? There is a name for someone like that: hypocrite. As I think back on it now, the adultery didn't really bother me; it was just a convenient place to hang my anger. It helped me avoid why I was truly angry. At the time though, I could not even admit that I *was* angry, let alone understand the reason behind it.

Along the way, certain friends made comments that were pivotal. One such remark was from Carolyn. "Christine, you are one of the nicest people I know. You go out of your way to help everyone. You open up your home to anyone who needs it. You are so giving, but you won't give your birthmother the time of day." I did not like this comment of course, but it did make me think. I have a great deal of respect for Carolyn and felt I needed to consider what she was trying to say. I repeated Carolyn's comment to another friend, Pat. She said, "I have always felt the same way. Why is this so hard for you?" As the saying goes, "The third time is the charm." I called Beth. I was hoping someone, anyone, would defend my character. I wanted to hear, "You are perfect just as you are." I told Beth what Carolyn and Pat had said. She hesitated for a moment and then said, "Yeah, you are nice and everything but what about your relationship with your brother?" She was aware of my history with Danny. I did not talk to him during my entire twenties. When I was near 30, he had married for a second time and had a son born with Down Syndrome. For a few years after, things were better between us. He was sober, holding down a job and working hard to provide for his family. I allowed him to stay in contact with me as long as he met the standards. A second divorce and a hard fall off the wagon led me back to silence.

I thought about what all three had said but in particular Beth's comment. I knew why I treated my brother the way I did; I was mad at him. If I treated my birthmother in the same fashion (withholding my contact), I must be mad at her too. Why?

*   *   *

One night Murph and I were in our neighbor's hot tub. (If you need to have a difficult discussion with someone, I highly recommend conversing while soaking in bubbly warm water.) I brought up the card I had received from my birthmother and my appointments with Jenny. I told him I was scared. I had dug my heels in so deep, for so long, I was afraid to think I was changing my mind. He told me it was okay if I were feeling different about the situation, he would support me no matter what.

I was still hesitant about what I was doing and why. I did need to face things, to figure out why this situation had been so hard for me for 15 years. I called my Aunt Barb. Even though she lived across the state, we stayed in close contact over the years. I felt our relationship had evolved from aunt and niece to friends and equals. I valued her opinion. She made a comment at one point, "You are a mother. Could you imagine giving up one of your children?" I did not say it aloud, but in my head, I rationalized the situation. I thought to myself, "Yeah, but I was married, we wanted a baby, and we had family support and resources. We made a conscious decision to have a baby. My birthmother did not have any of that." It was the first time I even came close to defending my birthmother.

I confided to Aunt Barb that I was nervous about telling my mother about pursuing contact with the north country people. I explained my interest was not so much about them, but about figuring out why this had been so difficult for me all these years. She encouraged me to be open and honest with my mother. Perhaps I was selling her short in her ability to understand my feelings. My mother told me many times over the years it was okay for me to be in contact with my birthmother. I did not believe her. I felt like even thinking about my biological family was a betrayal.

When I was first trying to figure things out, I had commented to Martha that maybe I would get in touch with Danny. Given our history, Martha suggested I think hard about that decision. My interactions with Danny did not usually lead to warm fuzzies for either of us. I told Martha that I felt he was the only one who could understand my hesitancy. Other adoptees I knew did not grow up with Mom and Dad and even though she grew up with the same parents, she was not adopted. Danny was the only one who could understand my feelings.

The next day I had an appointment with Jenny. It was a hard one. I talked about feeling like a hypocrite. I had kept people out of my life, namely my birth family as well as my brother because they did not live up to my ideals. I talked about holding them responsible for actions, negative actions, which were in fact, not very different from things I had done in my own life. I held my brother responsible for difficulties in the family. I finally started to see my inability to accept him for who he was actually caused a much bigger rift. He was an addict. For the first time, I accepted addiction was a disease, something he could not control. The things I had done, not talking to him for a 10-year period, ignoring him at family events, those were all things I *consciously* decided to do.

I had not accepted my birthmother because of her actions, getting pregnant, running from home, giving me up. The truth was, all she had done was seek out love, or what she thought was love. Wanting to be loved and validated as a person is probably the most basic of desires. We all look for it and many times, struggle to find it. I left my appointment feeling lower than the soles of my shoes.

I went to my parents' house later in the day. My dad was in the garage. He could see by my expression that something was wrong.

"Dad, I need to talk to you. Do you know that I got a card recently from my birthmother?"

"No, I didn't. What did it say?"

"It was a birthday card. I am so confused Dad. I don't know why this is so hard for me. I have been seeing a counselor, trying to figure it out."

"Like we told you all those years ago, it is okay with Mom and me if you want to meet her and get to know her."

"Dad, I am just figuring out that I have some anger. I'm not sure why."

"I can understand you are upset. I probably would be too. You have to understand though, the sixties and seventies were different times. There was great shame for girls who were pregnant without being married. It is not like today where it is so common and more accepted. I am sure that your mother did the best that she could in a difficult circumstance."

I was sitting in a chair and Dad was calmly leaning against his truck. Much like our conversation from 15 years earlier, he sounded like a sage philosopher. I voiced concern about my mom, would she be able to convince me that she too, was okay with everything. Dad told me that he and Mom spoke the night of the call all those years ago. They both agreed that I should meet my birthmother. I had to think that perhaps they were eager for me to meet her; it would be a chance to show that they had taken good care of me. Along the way I also wondered if my father's open attitude would be any different had my birthfather been the one to call me. Probably not, but still I have wondered. I asked my sister one time, "Be really honest, how do you feel about everything?" I smiled at her response, "All I can say, good thing they are boys." She told me she didn't know how she would feel if a "sister" suddenly appeared in my life.

Dad reassured me that everything was okay with my mom. She would support me just as he did. We embraced and I left without talking to my mother. She was busy with my nephew and I wanted her full attention for this conversation.

That night I went back to speak with my mother. She was watching a movie in her room. I lay on the bed with her and she asked why I was there. I started to cry. I cried for the next three hours as I told her about Jenny, about the books I read and about needing to face this situation. Repeatedly during our talk, my mother told me she had no regrets about her life. It was all as it should be. My mother is a person who grew up poor; she was fourth oldest of 10 children. When my mother was 19, her mother died. The family experienced many hardships. She wanted nothing more in life than to become a mother. After several years of trying, she was told she was not able to have a child. These were all things I thought a person might regret, not my mother. She was an amazing model of faith. In her opinion, life was just as it should be.

I had always trusted I was exactly where I was supposed to be. I never questioned that my parents were meant to be my parents. I did not have the same level of faith, however, when my birthmother returned. I did not think there was any way God had orchestrated that.

My car broke down on the way home from my mother's house. The next day I felt sick, completely exhausted. I cancelled work for the next two days and called to get an appointment with Jenny. I wanted to go to Jenny and come clean. I wanted to tell her all the regrets I had. I would confess that, unbelievably, I had made mistakes. In the months that followed, when I would talk with others about this admission, the fact that I was not perfect, people would inevitably question, "Did you think you were perfect?" I don't know that I thought I *was* perfect, but certainly, I had the feeling that I was *supposed* to be perfect. Over the years, when I told people I was adopted, many would tell me how special that made me. Repeatedly over the years, I was told that I was *special.* As a young child, I didn't understand what those people meant. I thought they meant that I had to be special, above and beyond what was expected. No room for error. Coming to this understanding did not mean it was easy to change.

I borrowed a car and went to the appointment. It was only 48 hours after my previous session with Jenny. I think she was surprised to see me. With a concerned look on her face she asked, "How are you?"

"I'm not feeling well. I am exhausted and confused. I went to talk with my parents and I am so confused. I told them that I am thinking of getting in touch with my birthmother. My father told me that it was okay. Talking to my mother was harder. I cried for hours. She kept saying she has no regrets. She has no regrets, my mother has no regrets. *I* have regrets about my life. I have not had a real relationship with my brother since we were children. I have let 15 years of my life go by without facing the situation with my birthmother. I had a difficult relationship with my late mother-in-law and now I see there were many times when I did not make it easy for her."

I did not say all the things I wanted to confess. I just could not allow some subjects to the surface. I kept them where they had been for years, buried way down deep. I cried through most of the session.

"It's not good, it's not bad; it just is what it is," Jenny replied to my big admission.

In frustration I silently questioned, I pay you for this? I pay you to sit there and not tell me the answers? To sit there and nod your head as I come to these epiphanies like you knew the answer the whole time? I didn't know if I disliked her or respected her that much more.

*   *   *

I went home feeling like the weight of the world was on my shoulders. I finally came to some important realizations and now I needed to decide what I should do next? One thing I knew for sure, Jenny was not going to tell me. I had to figure it out for myself.

That night I told Murph about the appointment. I said that I had planned to talk to Jenny about things in my past, the things I wished I had not done. I told him when it came right down to it; I did not think I could admit to those past mistakes. He offered to come with me to the next appointment for support. (Have I mentioned before that my husband is a pretty good guy?)

It was now Sunday afternoon and I was watching television. The phone rang and I looked at the caller ID. It was my brother. I answered and he asked, "Is today Mom's birthday or tomorrow? I always forget." I told him her birthday was the next day. Quickly I thought, I could tell him to have a nice day and hang up or I could try to talk with him.

I took a deep breath and said, "Since I have you on the phone, do you have a minute? Do you know what is going on with me?" I spent the next hour having an amazing conversation with my brother. (Recall 48 hours before this phone call I was sobbing over the regret of not having a relationship with Danny.) I asked him what he knew of the situation from 15 years earlier. His answer was, "Not much." I went through the history and caught him up to my current circumstances. I told him about the surgery, how scared I had been and how relieved we were when all went well. I told him about getting the letter, about trying to figure things out. I told him about the comments from Carolyn, Pat and Beth.

"I have been mad at you and that is why I have stayed away from you. Now I see there is a connection between my feelings for you and my feelings for my birthmother," I told him.

"I always thought you hated me," he said.

"I never hated you. I hated the things that you did and what they did to the family. I made a mistake though. I took the things you *did* and I turned them into who you *were*. I was mad at you for hurting us and most of all for hurting Mom"

"I wasn't trying to hurt anyone; I just had problems," he said.

It was difficult to end the conversation. I had not talked to Danny for 60 straight minutes since I don't know when. We told each other to take care and that we would be in touch soon.

Murph walked into our room a few minutes later. I asked him to find me a white towel. I was ready to throw it in and concede defeat. I did not think I could continue on this pace of emotional growth. It was going to kill me. An hour later, I called my sister to warn her that pigs might be flying by at any minute. She was confused by the statement. I told her I had just had an hour-long conversation with Danny and it had gone fairly well. She should beware of the flying pigs or at the very least, prepare for hell to freeze over. We both laughed.

*   *   *

With the arrival of Monday morning, I prepared for new week. I got the kids off to school and then left for work. My cell phone rang. It was my mother saying Danny was in the hospital. He had a heart attack. Danny was 40 years old but had a history of heart trouble. He made this ER run every few months. He usually stayed a day or two and then was home resuming his life. (If this were a movie, I am sure there would have been a crescendo of intense music right before this phone call.)

I called my sister to tell her about Danny. She too was on her way out the door for an appointment. We agreed to be in touch with Mom and with each other through the day. I spoke to my mom a few hours later. She said Danny looked okay; they were keeping him for observation. I spoke to my sister again later in the day. She confided, "I was really scared today. Of all the times that this has happened, this was the first time I really thought he would die . . . because you made your peace with him." "Whoa, whoa, whoa, a one-hour phone conversation does not peace make." I could not admit to her that I had the same scary thought earlier in the day.

Later in the day on Monday, I had an appointment with Jenny. I put it all on the line. "When I came here last Friday I intended to admit to my past mistakes. I couldn't do it. I left here feeling lower than the soles of my shoes. There are things in my past. I am not proud of them. I can't forgive myself," I tearfully confessed.

"If Jesus were standing right here in front of you, what would He say?"

"He would tell me I am forgiven." I was beginning to get it. I had to forgive myself before I could move on with any other issues. I went on to tell Jenny about the phone call from Danny and that he was in the hospital. Even she seemed surprised at how it all was unfolding.

*   *   *

Tuesday, after work, I met my friend Mary for munchies. We sat and talked about life. I filled her in on the latest developments with Danny and my appointments with Jenny. Over beers and potato skins, we tried to figure out the meaning of it all. I kept saying that I wasn't sure of what I was doing.

"What can it hurt you? If you meet her will it hurt you anymore than you have already been hurt?"

"You should write that down for me," I quipped.

"She doesn't have to be in your life. You can meet her, ask your questions and then decide if it is enough. The relationship does not have to be on a deep, deep level."

There was that word *relationship* again.

Mary admitted that until recently, she had been out of touch with one of her brothers for several years. She acknowledged that it was far easier to stay closed off, than to work on the problem.

"Here is to the 'closed-off' people," I said raising my glass.

I continued with all my arguments of but, but, but and blah, blah, blah.

"Are you still trying to punish her? Are you looking for someone to tell you don't do it?"

As we talked about Danny being in the hospital and the fact that I had not gone to see him, Mary offered, "If she or you or Danny were going to die tomorrow, would you fight for the opportunity to see them, or would you go, 'Oh well'?"

"That is another good one, be sure to write it down for me," I said, raising my glass once again.

We eventually knew it was time to go; we paid the bill and went outside.

"Hey, when you get home, write down all those pearls of wisdom from today and send them to me. I should ponder them when I have a clear-head."

With a slightly exasperated look she said, "Get in the car."

She found a pen and a pad of sticky notes in her bag. She scribbled and thought, scribbled and thought.

"I already know it exactly. I just can't face it," I admitted.

Mary wrote down my words and added, "You are more ready than you think!"

We hugged and she handed me the stack of notes. I did not look at them until I was home. At the very end, she wrote, "DO WHAT IS BEST FOR YOU!" If only she had written down what that was.

*   *   *

Throughout the day on Wednesday, I spoke with my mother and sister. Mom said that in Danny's examination they found an enlarged lymph node. He was going to have a biopsy later in the day. These situations with Danny had happened so many times over the years: car accidents, chest pains, dizziness, you name it. He always pulled through. It had been years since I rushed to the hospital to be by his side. In fact, I don't know if I ever did. When I did go to the hospital, it was to support my parents. At this point, it seemed better to go about my normal routine and just check in. If something significant happened, Mom would let me know.

Allison and I were out for our weekly line dance gathering. As we left the dance center, it was snowing. Everything was covered white and the surroundings were quiet and peaceful. As I drove, a phenomenal feeling came over my body. It felt like something washed completely over me. At the same time, I heard a thought, not a voice, a thought. It said, "Go fix it." I knew it was God talking to me, and I knew it meant I should go see my brother in the hospital.

I drove my daughter home and told Murph I needed to go to the hospital to see Danny. After 15 years of marriage and several family crises, I think Murph learned to expect the unexpected. He didn't blink an eye about my statement. In fact, he offered to go with me. I declined his offer and drove over to the hospital.

I arrived at 9:45 p.m. Danny was not in his room. The nurse said he was still in recovery from the biopsy. I sat in the hallway thinking about why

I was there and what I would say when I saw him. I wondered if I would recognize his girlfriend, I had only seen her a few times. I wasn't sure if the quiet time of reflection was helpful or pushing me over the edge, probably both.

I had a sense all of a sudden, that I should call my birthmother. I had even less of an idea of what I would say to her than what I would say to Danny. Like other times along this journey, I felt that my actions were not in my control. Something bigger than me was at work. I believe it was the hand of God. I went to the hospital lobby to use the computer to find my birthmother's phone number. Somebody else was on the computer. I waited. As I stood there in the hall, I noticed my brother's girlfriend walking toward me. I asked if he was back in his room. She said yes and then asked why I was there. I said I had come to see Danny. She told me she was going to get him something to eat. I was encouraged because I knew if he was hungry, he was feeling okay.

I walked into his room; it was 10:30 p.m. I had always thought Danny was handsome and when other women would tell me that he was charming, I could see their point. At this moment though, he looked terrible, his eyes were all bloodshot and he looked bloated. He was sitting up and complaining (another positive sign) but still looked ragged. He was 40 years old but looked much older.

"How are you doing?"

"Okay. They screwed up the timing of everything. First, they said I couldn't eat. Then they said I could eat, so I ate. Then they said I shouldn't have had the breakfast and I would have to wait until six at night to have the biopsy."

He lifted his arm to show me the incision where the doctor had just removed his lymph node. I pulled the collar of my shirt down to show the scar from my lumpectomy.

Things were quiet for a minute, uncomfortably quiet. "It looks like you want to talk, but you don't know what to say," he said looking in my eyes.

I took a very deep breath and looked at my shoes. "I am sorry. Everything that has gone wrong between us all these years, it was not all your fault. I have been hanging on to so much from the past and I am ready to let it go. I am sorry."

"Okay," he said, and after a short pause continued, "So where are you guys going on vacation this year?"

It had taken me years to get up the courage to ask for his forgiveness and he erased all the negative history with one word, "Okay."

We spent the next hour talking about camping and kids birthday parties. Danny asked if I had made any decisions about contacting my biological mother. I asked if he remembered being told he was adopted.

"Oh yeah, I was about 8 when Mom and Dad told me. I freaked out, big time."

"You couldn't have been 8. When you were 8, I was 5 or 6, and I knew before I was 5. Maybe you forgot and they had to tell you again. You *must* have known before you were 8."

He told me that maybe someday he would search for his biological family. It was the most we had ever discussed the subject in our whole lives. He was 40 and I was 38.

A nurse came in, stood by the dividing curtain and motioned to my brother's roommate. She politely asked if I was almost done with my visit. It was nearing midnight. I gave him a hug, something I had probably not done in years, and left.

*   *   *

It continued to snow as I drove home. Similar to when I left the dance center, I was in awe of the quiet and peace that surrounded me. A line from the movie *When Harry Met Sally* ran through my head. At one point, Billy Crystal's character says something to the effect of, "When you come to a decision about wanting to spend the rest of your life with someone, you want the rest of your life to start right away." I heard a similar thought in my own head; if you are going to fix your life, fix it right now.

I got home, went down to the computer and looked up my birthmother's phone number. I woke Murph up and asked him to call her. I told him I was not ready to do it but I was so full of guilt. I had left her hanging for the past 15 years. I needed her to know I was trying to work on it. He looked at me and said if I really wanted him to, he would make the call. He suggested, though, we wait until morning. Maybe he was right; it was after midnight. He went back to sleep and I stayed up not sure what to do with myself.

I fell asleep at 5 a.m. as Murph was getting up for work. Two hours later, I woke up barely having enough time to get my daughter out the door for school. I sat on the edge of my bed at 7:30 in the morning with the phone in one hand and the phone number in the other. I dialed. A woman answered. My heart was pounding!

"Is this Diane?"

"Yes?"

"This is Christine Murphy. I am sorry for calling out of the blue, I am sure it is a shock. I just need you to know I am trying to work on it. I don't know where it will go but I am trying to work on it. I am sorry it has taken me so long." I think I said all this in a span of four seconds.

I do not remember the specific conversation after that. I know she sounded calm. I tried to tell her about my brother and how we had a difficult relationship and God told me to fix it and I knew if I fixed it with him I had to call her as well. I can only imagine she wondered if I had gone off the deep end. I did not know if I was making any sense. The time was getting late and I needed to get the other two kids off to school. As abruptly as I had initiated the call, I ended it saying I would try to be in touch again soon.

As the kids got ready, I called my sister. I told her I had gone to see Danny the night before and I had called my birthmother. She said, "That's great, that is so what you needed to do for healing." It sounded like she had known all along. Why didn't I know? She ended by asking, "Didn't Danny think it was weird that you were there, especially at 10:30 at night?"

"He didn't seem to."

I called my parents and tried to tell them about the calls as well. When I tried to tell my mom about my visit to Danny, she was confused. Telling her that I had gone to see him at 10:30 the night before only confused her more. The last she had heard from him, he was going into surgery. I don't know that anyone called her when he was in recovery as it was so late. She was clearly anxious about his condition and once she heard me say I had seen him and he was sitting up and complaining she handed the phone to my father because she was too emotional to talk. I cried as I told my father I had gone to the hospital and made my peace with Danny. He told me he was glad. I tried to tell him about calling my birthmother, but I became too emotional and needed to end the call. Dad asked for no details about how it all happened. The end result seemed enough.

A few minutes later, my husband called. He wanted to know if I needed him to do anything. I think he expected I would want him to call my birthmother from his office. I told Murph I already made the call and it went well. He told me he loved me and he would talk to me later.

Even when you are in the midst of chaos, life has a way of reining you back into reality. In the previous 18 hours, I had made some serious decisions and taken some significant steps. I needed to put that aside and get the kids ready. I switched modes and made sure they both had breakfast, lunches and backpacks.

On the way to work, I called Mary. I told her what had happened with Danny and Diane. We joked about how powerful our "meeting" at the restaurant had been just two days before. I thanked her for her guidance and especially for the sticky notes.

*   *   *

The day I called my birthmother was Holy Thursday. I went to church that night with a renewed faith. When mass ended I asked the kids to wait for me, I wanted to talk to Father Marty. A year earlier, I had gone to confession talking about the times in my life when I had been judgmental and unforgiving. I was sorry for those things but unfortunately, in the past year, I did not do much to change. I felt I was making those changes now and asked the priest for absolution again. I told him, as briefly as I could, about the previous 24 hours. He asked me if I was going to meet my birth family. I told him I was not sure and I "still had a few things to work out." He looked at me and said, "I don't think you do. I think you are good right where you are."

I also went to church on Good Friday, Holy Saturday and the sunrise Easter service. It was as if I could not get enough; I hung on to every word the priest said. I commented to friends that I felt cleansed.

Our Easter celebration with my parents always takes place on the morning before Easter. Dad cooks a big breakfast and then we have, "The Big Money Easter Egg Hunt." Over the years, this egg hunt has become legendary. Dad hides a few dozen plastic eggs filled with money around the yard. Some have coins and some have bills, big bills. A few hundred dollars is up for grabs. The hunt takes on a "no holds barred" feeling. Adults have been known to push, not only each other, but also small children out of the way.

Danny, just out of the hospital, arrived late. I asked him to sit on the porch with me and I told him of the call to my birthmother. We were both a little teary. I spent years trying to avoid being alone with Danny but as we sat there, I prayed we would not be interrupted. That Saturday morning was the first time in many years, probably over 20 years we were all together as a family without a palpable tension in the air. Later in the day, we gathered again at a children's museum to celebrate my nephew's birthday. It was a banner day.

A few days later, I called my birthmother again. Initially, I felt like I wanted to make the call but after a moment I didn't know what to say. I rarely asked her a question and if she asked me questions, I felt uncomfortable. Obviously, this was not the recipe for successful communication. During our second or third call, she asked if she could send me a letter. I wouldn't consent; I didn't think I was ready. Previous letters had scared me, too much talk of past events and past feelings.

*   *   *

It was now spring break and I was home alone. The kids were all at friends' for the day. I was on the phone with my sister when the call waiting beeped. I clicked over and it was my mother.

"Danny was in a car accident on Route 29 just outside of town! Can you get there?"

"I am on my way!"

I clicked back over to my sister and told her what happened. I ran out the door grabbing my shoes but not taking the time to put them on, I drove over barefoot. The words Mary had used a couple weeks earlier, "Would you rush to get there if you knew something was going to happen," filled my head. I was indeed rushing. Rushing and praying Danny was all right.

I saw the police lights up ahead. My chest felt tight and my vision was a little blurry. I had to concentrate just to pull over safely. I jumped out of the car to see Danny standing by his car. He was standing, I could be grateful that he was standing. He had a stunned look on his face and an officer was looking over the damage. At first glance, I could see several dents and blown-out windows. I didn't see any blood, another thing for which I could be thankful. Danny's girlfriend and son were also there. Karen looked shaken but not hurt. Danny said he fell asleep at the wheel and when the car drifted off the road, he startled. He overcorrected and the car hit a telephone pole on the opposite side of the road. My mother pulled up a few minutes later. The police said there were too many cars already there and asked her to wait in the store parking lot down the road. My brother asked me to take his son to the emergency room. He did not seem to have any injuries but Danny wanted to be sure. I got my nephew into the car and called his mother. We turned around and headed toward the hospital. I stopped at the parking lot to check on my mother. She had a familiar look on her face, an expression I had seen way too many times over the years. Mom looked deep in thought, but I knew she was actually deep in prayer. In times of crisis, my mother turned to prayer. I told her I was headed to the hospital and that I was convinced everything was okay; having my nephew checked out was just a precaution. She shook her head as if she understood all that I had said but I knew better. Until she could lay eyes on my brother and see for herself that he was all right, nothing I said was going to register. We went to the ER and I left my nephew when his mother arrived.

I knew Danny had been on his way to the surgeon's office to get his biopsy results when the accident happened. I knew his girlfriend's daughter came and picked them up so he could keep the appointment. I knew the surgeon's office was one mile away from the ER. What I didn't know was if I should go. I was sure the biopsy was going to show cancer. My brother had been smoking for 25 years. As I sat at the light by the hospital, I made a decision. Instead of making a left to go home, I made a right and went to the doctor's office. I sat quietly in the waiting room next to my brother. I studied him and again thought he looked so much older than he actually was. Danny's hair was fully gray and the lines on his face indicated he had experienced more than 40 years worth of hardship. The nurse called his name and I told him that I would be waiting for him when he was done. For the next 20 minutes other people in the waiting room may have thought I was deep in thought. I spent the time trying to remember prayers, prayers I had recited hundreds of times in my life. This day they would not come to mind. Each time the door opened, I held my breath. When Danny finally came out, he looked relieved. He said everything was okay, no cancer. I was so shocked. I was so happy.

*   *   *

I went home and called my birthmother. I told her about Danny's accident. I told her I had said no to the letter because I was afraid. I told her she could send me a letter. It arrived a couple days later and contained some updated photos. I showed them to my parents. Mom looked at them and did not say much. Dad pored over them asking several questions about where each was living, what they were doing for work and how old they were.

My children had always known I was adopted. What they did not know was that I knew whom she was, where she lived and that she had found me 15 years earlier. Given the events of the past couple weeks, it seemed like the right time to tell them. The conversation took place over dinner. I said that several years ago I had been contacted by my birthmother, we had exchanged some letters but never met. I told them she had two sons. I told them I had been talking to her on the phone and maybe we would meet at some point. They took it all in but asked no questions as we ate.

The next morning my 12-year-old daughter wrote me a note and slipped it under my door. She was upset this was the first she was hearing of everything. She wondered how these people fit into the family. Did it mean this woman was her grandmother? She also wondered, since my brother was now divorced, was his former stepson still considered part of the family.

About an hour later she came upstairs and sat on the bed. We had a long conversation about the definition of family. I told her when you grow up adopted; blood relationships take on very little meaning. I explained, in my opinion, the real definition of family had to do with the role someone plays in your life. We spoke of "Uncle" Roy. Roy was my sister's best friend growing up. He lived up the street and spent many hours at our house. He joined in on family vacations and was present for all the holidays. He became like a little brother. In fact, Roy not only appears in many of our family pictures, he has his own album on the shelf just like Danny, Martha and me. He was my first babysitter when I went back to work after Allison was born. He watched her for the whole summer. He was 19 and dealt with cloth diapers and frozen breast milk like a seasoned professional. Roy is the godfather of all three of my children and it seemed natural to refer to him as "Uncle" Roy right from the beginning.

I explained to Allison that when I was little, we lived far away from all of our "relatives." We saw them several times a year but my neighbors filled those roles. They became my aunts, uncles, grandparents and cousins.

As far as my brother's divorce, I told her I would always care about his former stepson but I did not really consider him a nephew anymore.

Around this same time, a new deacon came to work at our church. One day he had a chainsaw by the altar for his sermon. I wasn't sure what to think. He went on to explain when he was very young he asked his dad what it was. His father replied, "It is a chainsaw, it cuts wood." As the deacon got older, he continued to ask his father about the machine. Each time, as the deacon matured and could understand more, his father told him more. It cuts wood when the engine turns the chain. It runs on gas and needs oil. The deacon ended with this statement, "You learn *what* you need to know, *when* you need to know it and when you are *ready* to know it." I was now telling the kids about Diane for the first time. I could see, as they were ready to know more, they asked more and it was my cue to share more. The chainsaw story also tied into something Jenny had said to me repeatedly. I would question sometimes why it took me so long to come to some of these realizations. She would calmly tell me, "You just weren't ready." It took me a long time to understand that "you weren't ready" was not equal to "you were wrong."

Definitions and terminology were pervasive themes in the adoption books I was reading. I certainly struggled with the vocabulary. I did not like if someone referred to my birthmother as my "mother." I really did not like if someone referred to me as her "daughter." I even had trouble thinking of her two sons as "brothers." I had siblings already. To say Danny was my brother and then say these other two men were also brothers seemed unfair. Danny and I had been through a lot together. As children, we were good friends and had many experiences together. All of a sudden to have these two "new brothers," felt like it belittled the relationship with Danny. I realize this does not make a ton of sense since a week or two before I did not really *have* a relationship with my brother.

Interestingly enough, my mom would often say, "How is your mother?" It made me feel uneasy. I wanted to joke, "Well since you are right here in front of me, I'd say you look pretty good today." Instead, I would usually give her a look and a sigh.

*   *   *

Over the next few weeks, I emailed many friends with the latest developments. I then took a huge step. In an email to my friend Kim, I was able to refer to my birthmother by her name, Diane. After I was able to write it, I began to be able to say it. There was still a pit in my stomach and a lump in my throat but I was able to tell people her name was Diane and her sons were Ray and Richard.

One of the reasons I was afraid to meet my birthmother was I did not want somebody looking at me and saying, "You like pizza? I like pizza too! We must be 'family'." Years earlier when I sent Diane photos, she wrote back commenting I had the same hands she did. It unnerved me. Jenny asked one day why that was so hard for me. Tearfully I admitted I was afraid to have anything in common with Diane. I was even more afraid of her taking credit for anything positive in my life. If I grew up to be a caring and compassionate person, it was not because it was genetic. If I grew up enjoying music, love stories and sports, I could not admit I inherited that from Diane. I felt I owed everything I had accomplished, everything I had become, to my parents. They had made me who I was, not her. (Sounds a little angry, yes?)

I spoke to my birthmother in mid-April and she told me she would be out of town for a couple of weeks. I asked for her sons' phone numbers and permission to give them a call. She seemed happy I wanted to contact them.

On a Friday night, I decided to call. The older of the two is Ray. I called the number and he answered. I explained who I was and asked how he was doing. About 15 years earlier, he had written me a couple letters, but that was the extent of our contact. He sounded friendly. He told me he was glad I had called and he was sorry if he ever did anything in the past that offended me. I explained he hadn't done anything I just wasn't ready before. A few minutes into the call, I had to smirk a little. Ray sounded just like my brother Danny. They had the same vocal tone and the same laugh. He told me he had been in Iraq with the Air Force and he was fairly certain he would deploy again by the end of the summer. We were on the phone for about a half hour; it felt comfortable and easy. At the end, he offered me his email but insisted there was no pressure to use it. The last thing I asked him was how he thought his brother would react to a phone call from me. Ray spoke of their differences and how Richard had always been more serious, more protective of the family. He wasn't sure what Richard would say.

A few minutes later, I called Richard's number. He answered and, like with Ray, I told him who I was and asked how he was doing. This call was definitely more difficult. It started with him repeating, verbatim, his call to me 15 years earlier. He was concerned about what I wanted. He wanted to know why I was getting in touch now, all these years later. I tried to explain about my mom and the "no regrets" conversation. I explained I had recently improved my relationship with my brother and I felt it was time to face the situation with his mother. He seemed skeptical and said he did not like the only reason I was doing this was to make myself feel better. He wanted to know why everything couldn't be more balanced between what I wanted and what she wanted. Why did I get to call all the shots? I didn't answer these questions. I quickly had the impression that nothing I would say was going to change his view of me.

"What should we think about you," he asked. I felt like I was being interviewed.

"Probably the same that Diane has wanted me to think of her. I am a normal person. My life has had its ups and downs. I have done some great things and I have made mistakes."

I could see he was very protective of his mother and her feelings. I eventually needed to end the call as the whole family was waiting for me in the car; we were late for a birthday party. He wished me well and told me to drive safe.

After I hung up, I thought of something I wish I had said to Richard. He kept asking why, after all this time, why had I contacted her now? I wish I had told him of her card to me. I think Ray and Richard both thought my contact came unexpectedly. I don't think they knew *she* wrote to *me*.

The next morning I called Martha to tell her about the calls. I tried to sum up their personalities. When I was done, I questioned, "Who do *they* sound like?" She laughed because she knew what I was thinking. Ray was like Danny and Richard was like me.

* * *

I began telling my story to anyone who was willing to listen. I went to a Billy Joel concert with my friend Rana. We had been friends for a few years but she had not even known I was adopted so I had to start at the very beginning. I was talking so much I think the only word she got in was a, "Wow!" every now and then. So much was changing for me on a daily basis I started to say to people, "If you haven't talked to me since yesterday, you don't know the latest."

Some days I would feel like I wanted to call Diane but after I had dialed I wasn't sure what to say. She always did 90 percent of the talking. During one phone call, she told me after they had found me in 1992, she and Ray drove to Plattsburgh to look in my college yearbook. It was the first time they saw what I looked like. During the calls, she was always calm. She would tell me about the weather, about her tasks of the day and plans for the weekend. I never said much. Ending the calls was almost more difficult than starting them. I never knew *when* or *if* I would talk to her again.

I did lots of reading during these weeks. Many times as I read, I would agree with what the author said. Sometimes I was sad I did not understand all of this earlier in my life. I began to journal about the situation. I didn't feel comfortable writing about my own feelings so I mostly wrote things from the books, statements that struck a chord with me. I learned about grief and guilt. I learned about loss and pain. I read about sadness and anger. There was that anger word again. Did I have anger? If I did, at whom was I angry and why?

Sometimes I would have flashbacks of sorts to things I had said long in the past. When Diane first found me, she had asked if I would ever share photos of myself from when I was young. I can vividly remember telling friends, "She wants a picture of me?? No f***ing way. You want to know what your child looks like when she is five, you keep her." Yet somehow, I did not know I was angry. (Can you say DENIAL?). Telling a story like this one to Jenny was always amusing. She would sit and nod her head knowingly. I would then say, "But you already knew that didn't you, because you are just so smart." She was smart. She knew I had to come to these conclusions on my own. It was hard work though, and there were times I was not sure it would be worth it.

Chapter 4

ALLOW ME TO INTRODUCE MYSELF

I continued to talk with Ray on the phone. Sometimes our calls would go on for hours. He seemed to understand the situation was hard for me. I don't know that he knew *why* it was hard, but he was willing to give me time and space to figure it out. When I mentioned to Jenny that it seemed to be easier to talk with Ray than Diane, she suggested I meet Ray first. Perhaps meeting him would help me become comfortable with the idea of meeting Diane. I thought to myself, *this* is why you pay a professional. I would have never thought of that on my own.

I called Ray the next day and told him what Jenny had suggested. I told him I was concerned that meeting him first would not be fair to Diane. He felt the same way. We both agreed our meeting was a first step to possibly meeting Diane, not in place of meeting her. I told him if we moved forward with the plan, I wanted to be the one to tell Diane, to tell her how it came to be and why. Ray and I firmed everything up and made plans to meet on Sunday, the day before Memorial Day, at a restaurant in Schroon Lake. It was as close to a halfway meeting point as we could find.

I spoke with Diane on Saturday to tell her of our plan. She admitted she wished I was ready to meet her but was glad I wanted to meet Ray. She was surprised we already set a plan and I heard her gasp when I said Ray and I were going to meet the next day. She was complimentary of Ray during our talk, telling me he was funny and a good storyteller. I felt a little bit like I was being set up on a blind date.

It was now Sunday morning. I gathered a few photos to show Ray, the house, the kids and my parents. I was nervous and jumpy thinking about what was going to happen that afternoon. My thoughts were interrupted by the phone. It was my dad and he was going on and on about my ex-sister-in-law calling and something about me reserving the wrong campsite for later in the summer. (Lisa worked for the reservation company.) We argued back and forth for several minutes. I insisted site 19 was the one we had a few years back, the one we really liked. He kept saying Lisa said site 19 was the little site up on the hill and that site 15 was the one I was remembering. My father and I rarely quarreled but by the end of the call, he had that tone in his voice, the one that made me feel 8 years old. This problem was not what I needed, not today. I had not told my parents about the plans to meet Ray. I called my sister in tears. She agreed with me that site 19 was the one we liked from several years back, the one at the base of the hill. We were both looking at the map online and felt we were right. I called my father back to plead my case, using my sister for back up. He did not bite. We argued some more and he eventually hung up without saying goodbye.

I called Martha back and told her I was sure that we were right and there was only one way to know for sure. I loaded the kids in the car and drove 45 minutes north in the rain to Schroon Lake. As I got off the exit, I looked at the Black Bear restaurant. I had passed it hundreds of times in my life, but had never been inside. My plan with Ray was to meet at 3 p.m. at the Black Bear. I entered the campground and asked the ranger if I could go look at a particular site. As I drove down the hill and around the bend, the kids and I began to read the site numbers, 11, 13, and 15. At the top of the hill, I saw a site with no number in the front. I rolled down my window and asked the campers for the site number. My heart sank when they answered, "19." I *had* reserved the wrong site. I called my sister back and tearfully told her where I was and what I had discovered. I don't remember exactly what she said but her voice was sympathetic. I drove the 45 minutes home and called my father. I told him I had just returned from the campground and Lisa was right; site 19 was the small one up on the hill. He told me that he had already asked her to cancel the reservation. When she did, she noticed another cancellation had just come in, site 57. It was also one of our favorite locations in the campground. Amazingly, it was open for the same two weeks we had wanted.

*   *   *

When Murph came home from golf, he took the kids down to my parents' house. They had agreed to watch the kids overnight. The kids did this often enough that my mom didn't even ask what our plans were. She probably assumed we were going to dinner or a movie. I didn't think I could see my dad without breaking down from our earlier disagreement. Murph returned home and we drove the 45 minutes north to the Black Bear. I took a deep breath as we got out of the car. We walked in and looked around. The décor was like most other Adirondack diners, wood planks on the walls covered with animal photos. There were only a few people there. I looked in one direction and then turned around to look the other way. A man made eye contact with me. He looked casual wearing jeans, a sweatshirt and a baseball hat. He stood up and stepped toward me. I had seen him in photographs, but I think I was still not 100 percent sure it was him. He reached out his hand to introduce himself.

"Hi. I'm Ray."

Weeks before when Diane sent the updated photos, the one of Ray was on the day he returned from Iraq. He was in his camouflage uniform. On this day, even though he was not in uniform, I could picture him as a soldier. His body looked solid, kind of like a fire hydrant. He had broad shoulders and I envisioned him protecting his unit of fellow soldiers.

We shook hands and then sat at a table. I wondered if everyone in the Black Bear knew what just happened. I was 38 years old and for the first time ever, I was within arms distance of a blood relative. I could not bring myself to look at him. Every once in a while I stole a glance. Ray and Murph talked about sports and cars. I rearranged my silverware and spun my glass in circles. Was this really happening? Was I really sitting next to this person? We ate and I was able to make a few comments here and there. Murph was so great. He was quiet when Ray and I were talking and then added to the conversation when he knew I was struggling. After an hour or so, I asked Ray if he wanted to drive up to Schroon Village and walk around. We drove up in our separate cars. Murph told me I was doing a good job and he thought things were going well.

At the village, I told Ray how I came to know so much about this little town. While growing up I had vacationed at Schroon Lake almost every summer. It was a place that felt like home. I showed him the town beach and told stories of swimming, fishing and skiing. As we walked through the town park, our conversation turned a little more serious. He asked questions and I tried to explain how I didn't really know why this was so hard for me but I was trying to work on it. I told him about Jenny and trying to understand about the anger. He asked what I was angry about and I had to admit I honestly did not know. I told him about going to her office that first day with all the letters in hand. With a wry smile he eventually asked, "If you weren't interested in us why did you keep the letters all these years?"

I pointed at him, grinned and said, "If I knew the answer to that I probably wouldn't need to see Jenny."

As we walked through the park, I felt at ease with Ray. He was so accepting. If I were in his shoes, I don't know if I could have been as patient. I asked Murph to get my camera from the car. He took a picture of Ray and me with the lake in the background. We walked back up to where the cars were parked. I looked at Murph and said, "I don't know if I am ready for this to be over, can we stay?" He said yes and we invited Ray to stay and have a snack at the tavern. We ordered beers and snacks and visited for two more hours. I was more at ease. I was surprised at some of the things we discussed. He wanted to know my middle name and if I was right-handed or left-handed. The conversation was a bit unbalanced; for every 10 questions Ray asked about me, I only asked one or two of him. He was clearly more interested in my past than I was of his. I started to consider that while there was little information about adopted children being found by birth parents, there was even less about the impact on birth siblings. Ray had known about me and wondered about me for over 20 years. The conversation would take its serious turns and then go back to chitchat. Eventually, I looked at him and said, "We could probably sit here for several more hours but I know you have a longer drive than we do and it is getting dark." He agreed. We walked out to the cars to say goodbye. I thanked him for coming. He told me he was glad to meet me and hoped to see me again soon. We looked at each other and reached out to embrace. It was emotional.

*   *   *

Feeling pretty high on life and all proud of myself, I went for an appointment with Jenny. I told her how great it was, Ray and I spent six hours together and we talked about many things. I told her there was a lot to say and it might be better for her to ask questions. I might not get to something she wanted to know.

"Okay, did you ask Ray any questions about Diane?"

"No."

"You were with him for *six* hours and you didn't ask any questions about Diane or what she was like as a mother?"

"No."

"Why didn't you ask anything?" I could tell from her tone and posture she obviously thought that was significant.

I was silent for a moment or two. I wanted to get up and leave. This is too hard. This is torture. I am paying for this torture. Luckily or unluckily, depending how you look at it, I had too much respect for Jenny to leave before my time was finished. I trusted she would not lead me somewhere

I was not ready to go. I took a breath, "Because to ask questions about someone, to be interested in them, it means you care about them and I cannot bring myself to admit I care about her." I saw Jenny's expression, the one I had come to recognize as the "now we are getting somewhere" look. I was not interested in going any further down that road. I told her about talking with Ray and how I don't know why I am so angry. I raised my voice, "What am I so angry about?"

She patiently told me it might not be just one thing. It could be a combination of things. With that comment, I noticed it was time to go. Thank God for small favors!

The next day I went back to the library. I was surprised when I sought out the book about the broken inner child. The book I rushed back to the library, because I could not stand to keep it in my house just weeks before. I didn't drive there with the intention of getting that particular book; it was another time that I felt compelled by an outside force.

Ray called later that day to invite my family to an open house on the air force base in Burlington. I told him I had to think about it and would get back to him. Murph was going to be away, so it would just be the kids and me. I weighed the decision heavily. I just met Ray the week before and now he wants me to attend a "family event" at the air force base. What happened to taking things slow? I talked to the kids and told them of the offer. They were all for going. If only I could be at ease, the way they were. I called Ray after dinner and let him know we would be there. He informed me he needed to put our names on a guest list and our relationship to him. He told me he would be listing us as his sister, nieces and nephew. I didn't know what to say. It certainly would not have been my choice, but I was not in control of the situation.

*   *   *

Earlier in the day, I had called Mary. I wanted to talk about the appointment with Jenny from the day before. I asked if I could come to her house, I really wanted to talk in person rather than on the phone. I arrived around 8:30 p.m. and we sat out on her porch. I told her about the open house and that we were going to go. I said I was uncomfortable with Ray listing us as family relations.

Mary looked me in the eye and said, "Honey, just because you can't say it, doesn't make it not true." Why did she have to be so damn wise? She offered to make a pros and cons list about meeting Diane. On the pros side, I said perhaps I could regain some of my sanity. Mary did not rush to defend my mental status. I also said my friends and family could relax a little. The previous few weeks had been rather intense. When she asked about the cons, I could not think of one.

"There's your answer!"

"Mary, I feel like I am in the deep end of the pool and I don't know how to swim."

"I feel like you are hanging on with all your might. I want to walk over and scrape your fingers off the edge of the pool. Swim already!" It was such an emotional night and I was feeling drained. I thanked Mary for her time and her guidance and then drove home.

I did not sleep that night, something that was becoming a terrible habit. At 2 a.m., I went to the car and brought in *the book*. The author recommends reading the book slowly, under the supervision of a therapist and journaling after each chapter. I am sure the average person needs so much guidance, not me. I proceeded to read the entire book, cover to cover in a two-hour span. Of all the epiphanies I would experience on this journey, this was the most pivotal. It was after 4 a.m. and I sat bawling my eyes out. For the very first time in my life, I could see the answer. I was able to sit there and aloud say, "I am hurt and sad and angry because I was left." Once that came out, the floodgates were open. Jenny was right, I was angry about more than one thing.

I was angry that I had no idea who took care of me for the first 10 weeks of my life. I have had babies. I know how much work it is to care for a newborn. There was a family out there somewhere who provided me with care during those weeks and I had no idea who they were. I had never before thought of those people. In fact, I often feel like the first 10 weeks of my life did not happen. I have always thought of May 29 as the first day of my life, the day I went to live with my parents and my brother. My children have dozens of people in their lives who can say, "I've known you since the day you were born." There is *nobody* in my life who can say that! Not one person can say they have known me all my life.

Some of my anger was also aimed at society. I know my parents did all they could and all they thought they were supposed to do. Still I felt upset that while growing up we did not discuss the loss and grief associated with adoption. It was always presented as a win-win situation. I needed a home they wanted a child. Voila, everybody is happy.

What I had come to understand in these months was all three sides of the adoption experience happiness, loss and grief. Diane may have been able to place me in a better situation than she could have provided but that didn't remove the pain she felt in not being able to raise me. It was a pain she would feel each time she was asked how many children she had or each time she saw a girl my age.

I grew up in a great home but that did not erase the fact I lost all that was familiar to me on the very first day of my life. I am a mother. I know my baby knows me even before it is born. My baby knows my smell, my voice and the rhythm of my heartbeat. I can picture myself as a newborn. I go through everything to be born and then all of sudden there is nothing familiar or comforting. I have always been independent. After thinking about this information, I could actually see myself, perhaps at two or three days old, saying, "Where did she go?" When no answer was provided, I can imagine I said, "Well I guess I'm on my own." I lived with a foster family for a couple of months and just when I am building up some trust there, I am moved again to a place where no thing or person is familiar.

For my parents, adoption did not eliminate the fact they were not able to have a child of their own. I can only imagine the insecurity people feel when they are not able to conceive or carry a baby to term. My mother talks about being pregnant with my sister. She had tried for so many years yet no baby grew inside her. For all the months when her figure changed, when she felt kicks inside, and when she heard a tiny heartbeat, she never really let herself believe she would give birth to an actual baby. She has told me even after she pushed Martha out, she thought a nurse would come over and tell her there had been a mistake and she really didn't have a baby. When I think of this, I am sad.

In these months I learned to appreciate information and understanding can come from a variety of sources. One day Allison and I participated in a mother/daughter workshop for young teen girls. A therapist began to read an essay written by an 11-year-old-girl. It was one of the most profound things I had ever heard. It would play an important role in my journey. The crux of her essay was that we are not just the age we are today. We are also all the ages we have already been. I began to see that as an adult, as a 38-year-old woman, I could understand Diane's actions. She was not married, did not have family support and did not have the resources to keep me. The 38-year-old in me understood all of that. The problem was, the 38-year-old was not who was actually hurting. The person in me who was hurt, sad, and angry was the one-day-old who was missing her mother. The one-day-old could not possibly understand. The one-day-old was feeling broken. I suppose that book was not the "load of crap" I had originally thought. So, there in the basement at 4 a.m., I had come to understand quite a bit about myself. Now what should I do? At 7:30 in the morning, I called Diane.

"I think I am ready to meet you."

"I think we should wait," she replied.

Her statement took me by surprise, and I suppose, impressed me. For the first time I felt like she was putting my needs ahead of her own. She had been waiting to hear these words all my life. She was concerned because of the comment I made about not being comfortable with her on the phone. I had not intended to share everything with her, but over the next

15 to 20 minutes, I told her about reading *the book*. I was able to tell her I was beginning to understand why this was so hard. I was able to see why I was angry. I told her I was sad and hurt and angry she left me. I tried to explain about the essay from the 11-year-old. Once again, I was not sure I was making a lot of sense. I could tell Diane was upset hearing all this. She was unusually quiet. I am certain it was painful. Needing to get the kids off to school, I ended the call saying I would try to call again soon.

I needed to tell Mary all that had happened since leaving her house only nine hours earlier. I knew I would see her at a school event later that morning and if I did not tell her everything ahead of time, I would probably burst into tears on the spot. I sent a note to her classroom. There were many other parents around when I first arrived. Mary and I did not even look at each other for a few minutes. Eventually we made eye contact and her expression said, "How did all of that happen overnight?" My eyes welled up and I looked away. After the event was over, we had a couple minutes to talk. I tried to tell her about the book and how I felt at 4 a.m. I told her of my call to Diane. We both needed to get back to work. We hugged and once again, I thanked her. As always, Mary told me she was proud of how hard I was working.

I called Diane the next day. I wanted to see if she was okay. I knew our conversation the day before was not easy. She told me it was hard to hear, but it was honest. She added that if our relationship stood a chance, we would have to be willing to hear the hard stuff too.

*   *   *

Saturday night I talked to each of the kids about going to Burlington. They all seemed fine, no big deal. If only I could be so calm. As I talked to Katie, the 7-year-old, she asked me when I first met Ray. I explained that it was only about a week earlier. Then she asked when I first met Diane. I told her I had not met Diane. I could see the wheels starting to turn, as she looked confused. She said, "How did you not meet your mother?" Luckily, my sister had a baby a few weeks before. I said, "You know how Aunt Martha pushed Sam out of her belly?" She nodded. I told her, "After Diane pushed me out of her belly I did not go home with her. I went to live somewhere else."

"With Gramma and Papa?" she asked.

I told her I lived somewhere else for a couple months and then went to live with Gramma and Papa. Her next question, "Who drove you there?" Oh to be 7 years old! She then asked whom Ray and Richard lived with when they were growing up. I told Katie they lived with Diane. I was blown away when her next question was, "Why did she keep them and not you?"

When I told her I was not sure, she simply said, "The next time you talk to Diane could you ask her?"

On Sunday, the kids and I went to Burlington for the open house. I was nervous. Ray met us at the gate. He was in his fatigues looking very official. We parked and went into a building where there was a reception. Ray introduced me to his superior officers, "This is my sister Christine." The sound of it made me uncomfortable, but not devastated, a sure sign of progress. It was a fun afternoon. We ate, played games, saw aircraft and watched military demonstrations. Ray needed to step away at one point. Katie turned around and when she didn't see him she said, "Mom, where did your brother go?" Why was it so easy for her? Why was it so hard for me? We drove Ray back to his hotel and standing in the lobby asked someone to take a picture of the five of us. It is a good picture; we all look happy. Before we left, I asked Ray if he would be available on Thursday. I wanted to know if he could meet me in Plattsburgh. I was ready to meet Diane. He told me he would do whatever I needed. Ray impressed me. He found a way to support me in my hesitancy and his mother in her excitement.

I called Diane and asked if she could meet on Thursday afternoon. She agreed. I got off the phone feeling happy and excited. Within an hour, those positive feelings were replaced with anxiety and confusion. I had doubts about my ability to make decisions. I didn't think I could trust my instincts. I told a select group of people I made the plan for Thursday. Everyone was encouraging and told me it would all be fine. I didn't tell my parents. I am not totally sure why. I think in part because I still felt like I was betraying them.

My friend Bonnie joked, "If you say something so shocking (in a good way of course) that Jenny falls out of her chair, your session should be free." During my appointment on Wednesday, I almost qualified as I told her of all that had happened since my last session. I shared about my visit with Mary, reading the book until 4 a.m., crying in my basement and the phone call to Diane the next morning. I told her about going to Burlington and making the plan to meet Diane the next day. "Do you think I am ready? Wait! Don't answer that. Do you have any concerns about me going?"

"No, I don't. What is the worst thing that could happen?" She asked.

"I will disintegrate into a million little pieces."

"I can guarantee that won't happen."

"Is that a money-back guarantee?"

Our time was up. Jenny wished me well, gave me a hug and sent me on my way.

I was a wreck that night-I couldn't sleep. I stayed up most of the night working on scrapbooks I was making for Allison's softball team. I did anything to keep my mind off the trip to Plattsburgh. The kids went to school and I went to work. We were not going to leave until 12:30. I could not picture myself staying home; I would go crazy. My beloved job, providing speech therapy to children in their homes, would be my distraction for the morning.

On the way from one visit to the next, I passed my church. I stopped and lit three candles, one for Diane, one for my mom and one for me. I prayed that I was doing the right thing. I cried. I felt like I needed to tell my parents about the meeting. They knew just about everything there was to know about me. I couldn't imagine taking this step without them knowing. I went to their house. My mother was in the living room. I told her I was going to Plattsburgh to meet Diane. I started to cry. She asked, "If this is so hard for you why do you want to do it?" I told her I had to; I had to face it once and for all. I told her she was the one who said she had no regrets. I didn't want to reach a point in my life where this was my biggest regret.

She said, "Well just pretend you are meeting a neighbor." I started to get upset. I did not want to pretend anymore and I told her so. I confided I wasn't sure she was actually okay with everything. She reassured me she was. "Mom I have seen you over the years. You keep your mouth shut when you are unhappy because you don't want to 'make waves'. I have also seen you say things you don't mean. You tell people what they want to hear. How can I really trust you are telling me the truth?"

I tried to explain what I had been learning about grief and loss in adoption. My mom spoke about her insecurities as a young mother. My brother cried all the time when they first got him. He spit up a lot and was colicky. She said she cried all the time too because she did not think she was meeting his needs. Then I came along. She said I *never* cried, just sat and took in the world. This also made her cry because she thought I did not need her. We calmed down and my mother offered to go to Plattsburgh with me. While I felt ready to face things, I still didn't think having my mom meet my birthmother was something I could handle. I told her Murph was going and I would call her when I got home. I told her I loved her and we hugged.

Amazingly, my father had been in the backyard for this whole exchange. I went out and briefly tried to explain things to him. He also offered to go with me. When I declined, he wished me luck, hugged me and told me to drive safely.

I still had one more client to see before the trip. I went to Brian's house and attempted to play games with him. How I made it through those 30 minutes, I still don't know. Right after, Mary called to see how I was doing. I told her about going to my parents, and how I thought I made a mistake. I was upset and unsure about my decision. She assured me all would be okay.

I arrived home and gathered my materials. It was a two-hour drive so I figured I would keep working on the scrapbooks in the car. I needed more adhesive and went next door to my friend Stacie's house to borrow some tape. We talked the night before and I confided my fear of disintegration. She smiled as she told me she found something in her kitchen drawer for me. I held out my hand and in it, she placed a small tube of super glue. She told me I would be okay, but in case I wasn't, she would help me put myself back together again. I felt lucky to have such supportive friends.

Another friend had sent me St. Theresa's Prayer in an email. The first two lines were powerful given my plan for the day. "May today there be peace within. May you trust God that you are exactly where you are meant to be." I printed it out and on the back wrote the names of 20 people who I knew would be spiritually with me in Plattsburgh. I put the paper in my pocket with a small crucifix and an engraved pewter stone that said, "forgiveness." I had carried those two items with me since the beginning of Lent.

*   *   *

I worked on the scrapbooks on the way up. I surprisingly slept a little bit too. When I woke up, we were getting off the highway. Plattsburgh is where I went to college and where Murph and I lived for the first year of our marriage, it was familiar and comfortable. We drove down through town and past our first apartment. As we pulled into the parking lot of the restaurant, another car pulled in at the exact same moment and parked along the passenger side of our car. I was petrified. It was not the Jeep Ray had at our previous meeting. I suddenly remembered that Diane had someone drive her so she would not have to be alone.

"Is that them?" I nervously asked.

"I think so."

I could see Ray in the back seat of the car. I had been sleeping in our back seat and was still there. I consciously got out on the driver's side of the car so I would be with Murph. I stepped out of the car and Ray came around, shook Murph's hand and then hugged me. Everything started to get fuzzy. I felt sick. My breathing was way too fast. I couldn't see so well. I started to cry, hard. Ray introduced Diane and she took my hand in hers. I couldn't look at her. I started to sob. I thought I would pass out.

Diane said, "Do you think you need a minute?" I shook my head yes and she and Ray stepped away. Murph held me up as I leaned against the car. He told me he loved me and everything was okay. I found myself in unfamiliar territory. I felt out of control. During emergencies, I typically hold it together and can easily take action. During this initial moment, I was completely overcome. When I calmed down, I told Murph

I needed to splash some water on my face. I went into the restaurant bathroom and looked in the mirror. I didn't look so good; my face was tear-streaked, red and puffy. My eyes couldn't even open all the way. I washed up with cold water and felt like I could breathe again. Murph was waiting for me outside the door. As we turned the corner, I could see Ray and Diane were seated at a booth. We walked directly over to the table but in hindsight, I wish I had taken a minute to stop and look at Diane without her knowing. Up to that moment, I only had a split second impression. She seemed young. I always have to remind myself that she is over a decade younger than my mom and dad. I also wondered how she was holding it together. Diane had pursued me for so many years. Our meeting today was what she had wished for all my life, yet she appeared so composed.

"Murph please sit on the inside. I can't sit across from her. Please sit on the inside?" He agreed and we sat down, everyone was quiet. The waitress approached and we ordered drinks. Thank God the waitress had gaudy makeup and body piercings. Her questionable taste in fashion became the first topic of conversation for the other three people at the table. I said nothing. I rearranged my silverware and folded my napkin. I could not look at Diane. Murph, Ray and Diane made small talk about weather and traffic. I rearranged my silverware and folded my napkin.

I wanted to be more together. I wanted to be part of the conversation. It was another time in my life when my brain and my heart could not synchronize. I kept stealing glances at Diane, praying that she would not be looking at me in that same nanosecond. It seems silly to say, but she looked like a regular person. I listened to the sound of her voice. Even though we had several conversations on the phone, hearing her speak in person made an impact. She was a real person.

"I haven't eaten anything today and maybe I should order something. Maybe I'll feel better." These were the first words my birthmother heard me say in person. We ordered food and quietly waited. I eventually handed Murph some photos to share. I had pictures of the kids, our house and my parents. For the first time, Diane saw the faces of the people who raised me. I did not see her reaction because I still could not look at her. When there were breaks in their conversation, I rearranged my silverware and folded my napkin.

After we ate, Diane left the table for a few moments. Ray looked at me and said, "This is harder than you thought?" I nodded yes. He asked, "Is there anything I can do to make it easier?" I shook my head no.

"Maybe we could go somewhere else. Somewhere where we could move around?" I asked a minute later.

"We'll have to call our friends back to get us."

"You can ride with us. I knew that suggesting we leave would mean you would ride with us. I'll go clean out the back seat."

Murph and I went out to arrange the car. Ray followed us out to have a cigarette. After a few seconds, I saw him hurry back inside the restaurant. He later shared with me, that he realized Diane would come out of the ladies room and see the empty table. When he got back inside, she was upset, actually more than upset. "Are they gone? Is that all I get?" she cried. He told me that she was leaning against the wall looking like she was about to pass out. Ray calmed her down and explained that we just wanted to change the environment. When Ray told me her reaction, I felt terrible. I did not think about what it would look like from her perspective.

As we drove back uptown, I pointed out our old apartment, my old dorm and the building where I took most of my classes. Diane was seated behind me; I could not see her. I think it made it easier. I felt like I was talking to myself.

When we went into the mall, I suggested Murph and Ray walk ahead leaving Diane and me alone. I knew if I kept allowing the two men to carry the conversation I would never say anything. They walked off and we sat at a table in the middle of the mall. I don't really remember specific things about the conversation. She talked a little more about my birthfather and his children, two boys and two girls. I explained about seeing my parents that morning. I told her how hard it had been. She asked if I felt meeting her was a betrayal. I cried and nodded my head yes. Diane spoke about her late mother at one point. I commented that many years ago, I had received a birthday card from her. Diane was obviously stunned. She had no idea her mother had ever communicated with me.

As we sat at the table, someone walking by recognized Diane and stopped to chat. She spoke for a moment and then introduced me, "This is my friend Christine." I could feel my whole body tense up. How could she do that? How could she tell this person I was her *friend*? Thank God she didn't say I was her daughter, I might have spontaneously combusted.

Murph and Ray checked on us a couple times. Eventually I knew it was time to go. I wanted to get home in time to put the kids to bed. I looked at Diane and said, "As hard as this has been, I am not sorry that I came." She asked if we could take a picture together. I hesitantly agreed saying Murph had to be in the photo. I knew I could not stand next to her. Ray, Diane, Murph and I posed as one of their friends (the one who provided the ride) took the pictures, one with her camera, and one with mine. When I saw the picture, I looked like I was about to throw up. I studied the photo looking for physical similarities. I had done this with other photos of Diane but this time it was different looking at the two of us standing only a few feet apart. We were about the same height and there was no denying that our eyes matched. I could only do these comparisons for a few seconds at a time.

Before we parted ways, Diane handed me a basket of flowers and shook my hand. I am sure she said something as we left but I don't remember what it was. When Murph and I got in the car, I reclined the seat and tried to concentrate on breathing. I felt like I had just held my breath for three hours. I called my sister and said we were on our way home. When she asked how it went all I could say was, "It was really hard." I also called Jenny. I expected to get her voicemail and was surprised when she answered. I told her it was over, it was hard and I was exhausted. I slept for an hour or so after that. I called Mary and her reaction was difficult. When I told her it was hard, she sounded so disappointed. I knew she just wanted it to go well and for me to be happy.

When we arrived home, I thanked my father-in-law for staying with the kids. I called my parents to tell them I was home. I put the kids to bed and talked to each one about meeting Diane. Katie listened and didn't ask any questions. When I asked Cole if he had any questions, he surprised me saying, "What was her personality like?" This was my 10-year-old son asking what I thought was a grown-up question. I said the first thing that popped into my head, "She seemed nice." Allison had more questions. She did not like that I went without telling her. I explained that I knew she would be concerned for me and I needed to focus all my energy on the meeting. I did not want to worry about her too. I was able to explain more of it to her saying it had been hard and overwhelming but it was something I needed to do. It was the hardest thing I had ever done. Nevertheless, I had done it and Jenny was right, I did not disintegrate into a million pieces. By the time we got home, I already knew I would try to see Diane again. This first meeting was just that, a first meeting.

I would tell the story of our first meeting several times. At the end I would always add, "If nothing else comes of this, I have discovered just how much I love my husband. He was so supportive and just amazing. If you see him, be sure to tell him you heard his wife loves him."

* * *

The next day, between work visits, I called Ray. Then I called Diane. I was concerned about how she was. The day before probably did not go as she had hoped. On talk shows, adoption reunions are portrayed as fun and easy. Everyone hugs; they compare birthmarks and mannerisms and live happily ever after. Our day was not like that. I spoke to her briefly. She sounded distant and tired. I told her I was sorry about walking out of the restaurant. I told her it did not occur to me that she would think we left. I told her I was really sorry about that. I also thanked her for paying for our lunch. In all the emotion, I had not taken the time to thank her. I felt bad about that too. After the call, I thought about my concern for Diane's well being. It had to mean something that I worried how she was doing. Could I possibly admit to caring about her?

Mary called to see how I was feeling. I told her that I was exhausted, emotionally and physically. I hadn't slept well and my eyes felt like they were going to fall out of their sockets. She told me that I was suffering from an "emotional hangover." What a fitting description.

On Friday night into Saturday morning, I participated in a Relay for Life fundraiser. The course was a quarter-mile track which I circled dozens of times. I think I covered well over 10 miles. It was probably the best thing I could have done. Sometimes I walked with people I knew but more often, I walked alone. I walked and thought. I realized when I met Diane on Thursday, I had become so overwhelmed in that first moment, and I just couldn't recover. Now that the initial meeting was behind us, I thought about the possibility of another get-together. I thought maybe once school was out and baseball and softball were over, I could have enough energy and attention to make it be a more positive time.

I had sent Ray the photo from Plattsburgh via email. He asked if I would send a copy to Richard and Diane. Before I met Diane, I resisted using email; it can be so impersonal. Now that we had met, it seemed a little better. The phone was still uncomfortable and regular mail takes so long. Email became a good compromise.

*   *   *

Mary and I had dinner after the last day of school. I showed her some photos Diane had sent. They were of Ray and Richard as children and young adults. We spoke about all that had happened. I wasn't sure how much more I could take. Sounding much like a philosophy professor, she offered this, "You have two choices; keep going on the journey or stop." I decided to keep going. Going through such emotional ups and downs was not only tough on me but my friends too. I was lucky to have so much support. One of the nicest comments came from my friend Linda. At one point she apologized; she felt maybe she had not been as positive about the situation as I would have liked. On the contrary, I felt she was fully supportive. She said she had reserved some of her opinions because it was *my* journey. She said, "I wanted to see where you would go and I would follow." I found that to be an amazing show of faith in me, a faith that I would find the right path.

During a phone conversation, Diane spoke about the quilt she had made for me. I told her that it was too large for any of our beds. She asked if I would like to give it back and she could alter it. I consented in a very wishy-washy, "It doesn't really matter, whatever," comment. I could not admit to it at the time, but I was grateful I had listened to my sister and not given the quilt away.

I suggested a second meeting at a wildlife museum in Diane's hometown. We agreed on a date just over two weeks from the first meeting. The night before I left, I talked to each of the kids about going. Allison was uneasy. I reminded her of a recent homily from our priest. He talked about having trust in the plan. Father Marty talked about people coming and going from our path throughout life and we had to trust they were there for a reason. I told Allison I listened very closely to those words as I felt they were directed right at me. I shared with her that I have always felt I am exactly where I belong. I never doubted my mom and dad were supposed to be my parents. Unfortunately, I did not trust God when Diane came back onto my path 15 years earlier. I told her I needed to figure out why that happened. She seemed to understand.

Ray agreed to meet me for breakfast before I went to the museum. It was the first time I met his wife and his daughter. They were very welcoming and we made conversation easily. His daughter was only a year or so older than Allison. As we ate Ray joked, "Hey I just realized I am the middle child now. I don't have to be the oldest anymore." This type of comment made me uncomfortable. In my head I would usually respond, hold your horses there Buddy. Just because we have met does not make us brother and sister. Ray and Richard had known about my existence since they were young children. For them it was a done deal; I was their older sister. When we walked out of the diner, Ray pointed to the street corner telling me Diane's house was the third one down. It is a small town. I think he was teasing me knowing how anxious I was feeling. Diane and I had agreed to meet at the museum so I stuck to the plan. I drove across town and found the center. As I walked to the front door, I could see Diane getting out of her car. She was calm and smiling. Someone passing by would probably think we were old friends meeting for an afternoon visit. I didn't cry and I didn't feel like I was going to pass out, definite progress. We went inside and began to walk around. It was so much better than the confinement of the restaurant. Eye contact was still an issue for me. I walked ahead or beside Diane, never turning to talk directly to her. I kept my attention focused on fish, otters and turtles. I definitely have a thing for turtles.

A mother snapping turtle comes into our yard each year in early June and lays eggs. About three months later, if the nest were not destroyed, we usually find a few surviving babies. Something about the turtle tank at the museum made me feel calm.

Diane suggested that we take a walk on the nature trail. She told me more about her extended family. I felt like I should have been taking notes. I was having enough trouble keeping track of Diane, Ray and Richard's histories. Stories of aunts, uncles and grandparents went in one ear and out the other. I talked about my parents and their siblings. I shared that I was one of over 50 cousins on my mother's side of the family. Diane seemed to be eager to hear anything I would share. When she asked a few questions, I was able to answer with less anxiety than I had in previous conversations.

We agreed to leave the museum for lunch. Diane asked if I wanted to ride with her or drive on my own. It didn't make sense to take two cars so I rode with her. She showed me around the small town pointing out where Ray and Richard had gone to school and where they lived when the boys were young. At one point while she was driving I thought, she could kill me and leave me in a field at the edge of town. I, of course, did not feel a physical threat of violence but it spoke to how exposed I felt being alone with her. After lunch, we stopped by her house. When Diane offered for me to go in, I couldn't do it. I was afraid. Over the years I had sent a few photos, I was afraid to see them on the walls of her home. To me that was a privilege reserved only for my parents and family members.

We returned to the museum for another hour or so. I had taken many photos during the day and slowly worked up the courage to suggest to Diane that we find someone to take a picture of us together. A museum employee was near by and I asked her to take the photograph. I did not have my husband as a buffer this time; I had to be right next to her. I "smiled" as best I could but I know my expression still conveyed uncertainty. Afterwards we made our way to the parking lot. I thanked Diane for her time and told her I was glad I had made the trip. I am quite certain she was hoping I would embrace her but I just was not ready. I offered my hand and she took it in both of hers. At the last second, I remembered about the quilt. I drove my car down next to Diane's and handed it to her. I watched as she took it into her arms like a long lost friend.

Over the course of the day, Diane had invited my family to the town fireworks on July 3. Ray would be there, as would Richard. It would be the first time the kids could meet Diane as well as Ray's wife and daughter. Would it be too much to have all of us meet Richard for the first time on the same day? How could I possibly control the actions of all those people?

*   *   *

The next day Murph, the kids and I made a trip to my brother's house. It was the first time I had been there since he moved in a year earlier. He was hosting a picnic of sorts to celebrate Father's Day, our father's birthday and our parents' anniversary. Similar to how I felt at Easter, it was a day without tension. We were all at ease. I spoke with Danny privately about going to see Diane the previous day. I shared photos of my birth family with him. He told me he was happy for me. He told me he was happy too. He had a job he liked, a house he was proud of and a woman who loved him. As we sang happy birthday to my father I took a photo of him with his six grandchildren. It is a cherished memory.

Later in the week, I went out for the evening with my friend Rana. She was very gracious as she sat and listened to my ongoing chronicle. I spoke a great deal about my trouble with the names of the relationships. As a society, we qualify whom people are when we speak of them. Each person has a name, but he or she also has a qualifier as part of his or her introduction. "This is Joe, his daughter played on Katie's soccer team. This is Sue; her son goes to school with Cole." I was still having trouble with that qualifier piece for the members of my birth family. It had taken 15 years for me to use Diane, Ray and Richard's names. I would need more time to assign them a role. Rana has a variety of relations in her family. She has half-siblings, stepsiblings, a stepmother and numerous grandparents from the variety of marital unions. Her stepfather adopted her when she was 18. Two years later, her biological father and her adoptive father both died around the same time. She understood about the challenges of loss and grief. She had not been in touch with her father for some time when he died. We spoke about regret. I poured my heart and soul out to Rana that night. I made admissions about my past and the things I wish I had done differently. With the help of Rana and my other friends, I learned that nobody else *really* cared about my past. That was all it was, my *past*. I realized the only person holding it against me, was me.

Richard and I continued to have our challenges. I had a lengthy phone conversation with him about the possibility of my family attending the fireworks. I told him I was concerned it would be too much, meeting everybody all at one time. His response, "I am comfortable in my own skin so it is not a problem for me. If you think it will be too much for you and your family, don't come." I was getting used to these exchanges and I didn't let it ruffle me. We went on to talk about how I had been feeling sick and run down, not a shock with everything I had been going through. He asked if that was my body's typical reaction to stress in my life. He wanted to know if I "always overcomplicate things." I was pretty certain being found by your biological family and then waiting 15 years to meet them qualified as a complicated situation. We began to talk about my perceptions and in particular my definitions of family. At one point, he talked about me as his sister.

"I don't really think about it that way. In my opinion, family relations are made by commonality and shared experiences. The fact you and I were blood relatives means very little to me."

"Then what am I to you, just another one of Diane's sons?" Frankly, I could not have said it better myself.

Over the next few days, my circle of people suggested that we go to the fireworks. Many pointed out that I was the one who kept saying I had no shared experiences with Ray, Richard or Diane. In the end, I was able to set aside my own anxieties when I saw and heard excitement from my children. If they could be open to it, so could I. I called Diane and told her that we would be there. She would be meeting my children for the first time as well as hosting us all at her home. I don't know for sure how she reacted after that call but on the phone she was composed and acted like our visit would be an everyday occurrence.

*   *   *

I had a long talk with my mother the next day. I tried to explain to her about coming to understand why meeting Diane was difficult, coming to understand why I was mad at her. I asked her if she agreed you are all the days you have ever been. She agreed the 18-year-old in her still existed when she blushed at the thought of an old crush. She agreed my 10-year-old still has a 2-year-old inside him when he tantrums about more video game time. When I asked her, "Then do you agree there is a one-day-old baby somewhere inside me wondering where her mother went?" She was not overly convinced.

I asked my parents if they remembered telling me I was adopted. My mother looked at me confused. I told her I didn't remember being told. She said, "Well we did tell you." I had to laugh. Of course, they had told me, only I didn't remember it. When the subject came up with others I would always say, "I don't remember being told, it is just something I've always known." I thought I didn't remember because I was *so* well adjusted to the information, being told became an unimportant event. Maybe I was wrong. I think I blocked the whole thing out. After all, Danny clearly remembers being told; Martha clearly remembers being told; she was 7 or 8 at the time. Martha told me that she and Mom were walking downtown one day and Mom told a story that started, "When we got Danny and Crissy . . . ." Martha eventually asked, "Why do you say it that way? Why do you say that you 'got them'?" I had no recollection of being told I was adopted. Over the course of the discussion with my parents, I think they thought I was trying to blame them for not talking about it enough. "It's not like we walked around going 'Here are our two adopted kids.' all the time," my dad said. "Danny was our son and you were our daughter; that was it." My mother commented, "We did what the agency told us to do. We didn't keep it a secret. We told you when you were young but we didn't talk about it over and over. We didn't see the need to *keep upsetting you*." There was my answer, only my parents didn't or couldn't see it. Somewhere in the past, realizing I was adopted was *upsetting*.

*   *   *

Late one evening I was on the phone with my friend Bonnie. We were discussing what it must have been like the day my parents went to get me. How they walked into the building empty handed and walked out with a daughter. My mother saved everything. In my baby book were all the communications with social services. The stack of letters started with acknowledgment of their application and continued up to, "we have a girl for your consideration." The adoption agreement was also in the book. While Bonnie and I were on the phone, I started to look at all the papers. It was very emotional. This is what it says:

> *After careful consideration of the child and all that adoption involves, we receive in our home, from this agency the above named child.*
>
> *In doing so we agree that:*
>
> *We will care for this child, assuming full responsibility for the child's needs, including medical and surgical costs.*
>
> *We are taking this child with the intention of adoption although we understand that legal custody remains with this agency until the date of legal adoption.*
>
> *The legal adoption will take place after both the agency and we agree that it is in the child's best interest.*
>
> *In the period prior to legal adoption an agency representative will visit us and the child periodically and that we may call on the agency for consultation.*
>
> *If at any time prior to legal adoption it is determined by the agency or by us that the child should be removed from our home, we will cooperate with the agency in carrying this out in a way that serves the best interest of the child in the judgment of the agency.*

That was it; five little bullets of information, two signatures on the dotted lines and have a nice day. These days the contract for cell phone service is more involved.

*   *   *

On July 3, I worked in the morning. After one of my visits, I talked with the mother of my client. Kristin was aware of what had been going on. She was also a social worker so I sometimes bounced ideas off her. I replayed the conversation with my mother from the day before. When I spoke about the baby part, I was surprised by what came out of my mouth. "I was trying to get her to understand there was a one-day-old baby inside me who was confused. Everything that was familiar to that baby was now gone. I was trying to get my mother to understand the baby was sad and hurt because she was left. The baby felt like a piece of her was missing." I stopped talking immediately. Had I really just admitted to that? Kristin could appreciate what just happened. Tears welled up in my eyes as I kept repeating, "Did I really just say that? I have never said those words before in my life!" My head was spinning when I left Kristin's house. I called Jenny. I needed to tell her about what I had said. We spoke briefly. I told her my story and our decision to go to the fireworks. She wished me luck.

We left as soon as Murph was home from work. It was a two-hour drive and we arrived right around 7 p.m. Ray met us in the driveway and started introducing the kids to his wife and daughter as well as Diane. I was grateful that he was doing it, I was too anxious. We were only there a couple of minutes when Richard pulled in on his Harley. Like when I met Ray for the first time, seeing Richard in person, having a live face to put with the name and the voice was overwhelming. He was wearing a black leather coat and slick riding glasses. He looked tall, although I am only five feet tall so just about everyone looks tall to me. My moment of meeting Ray had been so private. Meeting Richard with everyone looking on felt as if I was under a microscope. I didn't see anyone else though, I was trying to focus on Richard. He walked over and I extended my hand to shake his. He took my hand in his and then proceeded to wrap his other arm around me in a hug. I was a bit in shock. Three months before this day I was not even in contact with my birth family and now, we were all together for a picnic.

Even though Murph was with me when I met Ray and Diane for the first time, the meetings still felt like one-on-one experiences. A few days before the fireworks, I explained to Ray that I was worried meeting Richard with so many others around would not allow for the same individual feel. I am certain Ray shared this with Richard. He was going to walk to the corner store at one point and he very purposely invited me to go along. As we walked, he asked how I was feeling and how the trip was. I talked about the kids, summer camp and vacation plans, overall pretty surface-type conversation. On the way back, I was talking about my recent wedding anniversary. Richard asked how long I had been married and I answered, "16 years." He stopped in his tracks. Perhaps I had impressed him.

When we returned, I went into Diane's house for the first time. I tried to take it in without staring. There were several photos on top of the entertainment center. Off to the side on a separate table I saw my wedding photo. Other pictures of my kids were there too. I felt a little queasy. Shortly after, Diane asked to take a photo of Ray, Richard and me together. I asked one of the kids to get our camera from the car. The three of us stood there in her living room as Diane and Murph snapped the pictures. I tried not to say anything. I don't think anyone wanted to say anything. It was obviously an emotional moment. Diane took several deep breaths as she looked through the viewfinder. For the first time, all three children she had given birth to were in the same room. I was 38, Ray was 36 and Richard was 34. I can only imagine what was going through her head, what was going through her heart. She took two or three pictures and then Richard invited Diane to stand with us too.

Before leaving for the town park Diane offered everyone a snack. I brought a rum cake to share. This rum cake is legendary at our house; it is Stacie's recipe. I knew it would help with conversation. My sister who writes for a newspaper had once written her Thanksgiving Day column about this famous rum cake. Everyone had a piece of the cake and provided rave reviews.

We went to the town park and found a spot for all of us to sit. The kids were playing with sparklers Ray had provided. I continued to talk with Richard about his job, his studies and his girlfriend. I didn't talk very much with Diane that night. I felt for her it was more about meeting the kids. After the town fireworks, we went down to a beach where Ray was setting off fireworks of his own. I had never seen somebody do this beyond firecrackers and roman candles. It was interesting to say the least. It was getting late and we decided to head home. I spoke with Richard about the possibility of getting together a couple days later. We were all saying goodbye and I could see Murph and the kids giving everyone hugs. I walked over to Diane and thanked her for inviting us. She told us to drive safely and I reached out and embraced her. It was the first time I hugged my birthmother. I had to pretend it was not happening. I needed to stay in control. I could not let myself go to that place deep inside, the place I had only recognized earlier *that* morning. It was the place left empty so many years before when Diane relinquished me. If I got emotional, it would be like admitting I missed her. I hugged her quickly, turned and walked to the car. We left shortly before midnight. The kids fell asleep before we were out of the town limits. Once we were on the highway, I allowed myself to relax a little and think about what had gone on that evening. As I thought about Diane, about hugging her, I smelled the sleeve of my jacket. I could smell her perfume on me. For a second, I tried to recollect if it was a familiar scent. I closed my eyes and slept the rest of the way home.

*   *   *

Two days later, I saw Jenny. I shared the photos from Diane's house. We talked about looking for physical resemblances. Amazingly, I did not immediately change the subject, something I would have done in the past. It was true we all had the same cheekbones and rosy cheeks. Diane and I certainly had the same eyes. Sometimes these discussions further reminded me I had little information on my birthfather. I had no pictures of him. I was not even sure of his children's names. Diane had said them once but I did not remember what they were. Now and again people would ask me if I intended to contact my paternal "siblings." As far as Diane knew, these people had no idea I even existed. I was not sure I could intrude on someone else's life that way. I remember quite clearly how I felt when Diane called me unexpectedly, and I did not want to do that to anyone. I also told Jenny of my plan to meet Richard later that afternoon in Schroon Lake. We talked about my previous contacts with Richard; how they had mostly been a power struggle. I think we were in competition for who had built the bigger wall. Ray and Richard's father left the family when Richard was a young toddler. They have had very little contact with him since. I began to see that much of Richard's defensiveness came from trying to protect himself. He too had been hurt by loss and grief.

I drove from Jenny's office to Schroon Lake. Richard and I met at the same restaurant where I met Ray. Over beers, pizza and steamed clams we contemplated the meaning of life. Along the way, I talked about what I had been reading about adoption and some of the struggles. I started many sentences with, "One book said that a lot of adoptees . . . ."

"Have you always worn your adoption badge so prominently?" Richard asked.

"No I don't think I have," I answered using a tone to show I was offended.

"So you just shined it up recently?"

"I guess you could say that."

This was not going as I had planned.

We started to talk about growing up. He asked about boyfriends, summer jobs and hobbies. I eventually got to the part where I failed out of college. He looked a little surprised. We talked about the perfectionist attitude we both seemed to share. I looked at him at one point and said,

"The problem with trying to live on that pedestal, when you fall, it is a really hard fall." He nodded his head in agreement and we bumped fists.

Our conversation continued and Richard said something that upset me. I don't even remember what it was. What I do recall saying is, "Don't go there. We've come a long way. Let's not go down that road." The conversation turned and we did not look back.

Richard talked about when Diane first told him and Ray about me. He told me that they never asked Diane any questions about who was the father or the circumstances of my conception. Ray had shared similar comments previously. Diane, Ray and Richard were all shocked, maybe even offended, when initially I didn't have any curiosity about them or the circumstances of my adoption. Interestingly enough, Diane told these boys about me over 25 years earlier, and in all that time, they asked no questions. A few days before, Diane told me she finally shared the identity of my birthfather with her siblings. She kept that secret for 38 years! She told me that once she told them, it did not seem like a big deal anymore.

I asked if Richard wanted to go up to the village. We paid the bill and went to the parking lot. I offered to drive and then he offered to drive . . . his Harley. He pulled a spare helmet out of his bag. I wasn't sure I wanted to ride with him, but I also felt rejecting the offer could be misinterpreted. I agreed to go but told him he could not tell Murph I had done it. I was in shorts and wearing sandals, not exactly the safest situation. As we went up the road, I felt vulnerable. It was not only my lack of protective clothing, but also the fact that I was putting my trust in someone I did not really know. I held on to Richard as we raced up the road, not too tight though. I didn't want to appear scared. We arrived, parked the bike and walked down by the beach. I repeated the stories I had told Ray about my childhood summer vacations at Schroon Lake. I added that my brother-in-law Martin proposed to Martha at the lake because he knew it was her favorite spot.

Richard looked at me and said, "So where do we go from here?" I knew he wasn't talking about our physical location. I told him I was hoping life could settle down a bit. I wanted to get back to my life. I had put so much on hold to try to figure things out. He said he understood, as there was much going on for him with school and work. He told me he hoped I would stay in touch. He asked if there were something in my life interfering with contact, to let them know so they did not have to wonder. We arrived back at the parking lot and I asked for his mailing address. When I put the pen and paper away, we said our goodbyes. It was emotional. He gave me a hug that overwhelmed me. I felt the power of it from the top of my head to the bottoms of my feet. I cried as I drove away. The next day, I received this email. I was amazed at how far he and I had come in only a few short months.

Christine,

I just wanted to send you a quick note before the hustle, and routine, of our lives pulled us back. I have to believe the timing of our meeting is coordinated by a power far greater than ourselves and that the same power will help us sort out what it all means. My hope is that the unsettled drive to reach out will be replaced by a new peace and an eventual comfort with us "north country people."

Even in our short time together, I am struck by how much I have learned about you and ourselves. It seems that each of us, in our own way, were able to open up. I heard stories I had never heard before. I really find significance in that. I am grateful for the communication that has drawn our tiny northern crew together.

Thank you for being so brave and sharing your family with us. I enjoyed meeting them all. Murph seems a fine man and I admire his support and patience. I am comforted knowing he is in your life.

Please take good care of yourself. I hope you catch up your sleep and continue to find the balance. Please don't hesitate to let me know if I can help. We may always be a little strange . . . but we will never again be strangers. Please extend my very best to your entire family.

Until then,
Richard

*   *   *

A couple days later, Ray was due to come to our area on business. I asked my parents, my sister and my brother to come to my house on Saturday to meet him. Danny had to work and was not able to commit to it. He told me, "Next time, I promise. I want to meet him." My parents, my sister and her family would be there.

Friday night Murph and I went to dinner. As we ate I said, "Have you ever had the experience where you said something, and until it came out of your mouth you had no idea you were going to say it?" He looked at me with a "What now?" expression. I said it wasn't anything bad. I went on to say, "I was talking to someone the other day and I was telling her how great you have been. You have been so supportive and so understanding. I said you have been so great you might just get a motorcycle out of it." He choked on his salad. I smiled and said, "Don't make me say it twice." About 15 hours later, he was signing the papers. After purchasing the motorcycle, Murph and I met Ray in Lake George for lunch and then went to the store to buy food for dinner. Back at the house, I gave him the grand tour. I could see him studying photos of me as a young girl. Everyone arrived. The first few minutes were anxious for me. I have to credit my dad with calming me down. He walked right up to Ray gave him a great big handshake and started asking him a million questions about the service and about his time in Iraq. I was able to settle down seeing the conversation was flowing. Everyone ate and seemed to enjoy the experience. My sister and her husband said their goodbyes telling Ray how nice it was to meet him and they hoped to see him again. My brother-in-law thanked Ray for his service to our country.

I did not know until several days later that my mother had taken Ray aside at one point. She held his arm and said, "If you want to know what Crissy was like as a kid, just watch Allison. The apple doesn't fall far from the tree."

My parents left next. I had survived. I introduced Ray to my neighbor Stacie. She had seen me through so much of this journey. Ray put out his hand to shake hers and she said, "That won't do." Stacie reached out and gave Ray a big hug. She had heard me for so many months talk of how he was so patient with me. How he talked to me on the phone for hours. How Ray had helped me so much. I imagine the hug was a "Thanks for being so nice to my friend" gesture. My brother called to see how the visit went. I told him everything had gone well and I was glad I had done it. Danny told me he hoped he would have the chance to meet Ray soon. I spoke to Diane later that night on the phone to say the visit between Ray and my family had been a good one and, maybe someday soon, I would be ready for them to meet her and Richard as well. Things seemed to be moving along in the right direction. Can you hear the warning music beginning to build?

Two days later, I opened the mailbox and I found three letters from Diane. They were addressed to my kids. The letters made me angry. I felt so invaded. How dare she overstep the invisible line I had drawn in the sand? I had talked to her on the phone two nights before. She never mentioned writing to the kids. She only met them one time; why was she writing to them? I showed the envelopes to Stacie. I had the right to open them right? I am not sure she agreed. I am sure she was rational and was able to guess they were harmless "I am so glad I met you" letters. She did say, "You are their mother, do what you feel is right." I opened the letters. In each envelope was a note and a rain check for smores. I felt the letters were too strong. She ended one with, "You are very special in my heart," and each was signed, "Love, Diane."

I called Ray and told him I was upset Diane hadn't talked to me before sending the letters. She had promised to let *me* call the shots. She told me *I* could be in control. I told him I knew I was reacting strongly and needed a few days to settle down before I talked to Diane about the letters. I called her a few days later and said the letters upset me. She replied by telling me she had promised the kids we would have smores after the fireworks and then we didn't have the chance. She was afraid the kids would not trust her because something she had promised did not happen. She told me she would try to be mindful of my feelings in the future. That did not sound like the "I will never do it again" I was waiting to hear.

*   *   *

Diane was aware of my appointments with Jenny. She even offered that if I ever wanted her to go with me, she would. The letter incident seemed a good reason to take Diane up on her offer. I sent her this email a few days before the appointment trying to let her know why I wanted to see her at Jenny's office.

Diane,

On the phone the other night, I mentioned I have been trying to put some thoughts on paper. This letter is the result. At first, I thought I would share it with you at the appointment on Wednesday but then thought it might be better for you to have time to read it and perhaps write down some thoughts of your own.

The past four months have been very significant in my life for many reasons. I feel there is much to be grateful for during this process. Relationships with family and friends are so much closer due to the care, concern and support I have been given. In particular, the relationships with my husband and children are stronger than they have ever been. I have always been a fairly independent person but this process has made me reach out for help and support, a valuable life lesson.

Another significant event was reconnecting with my brother. This process has opened up many really important discussions with my children about family and relationships. I have been able to have discussions with my parents, brother and sister, which have been really important and helped us all to connect as a family. I have had the opportunity to be the person seeking advice, not something that has been easy for me but so very rewarding. I have a better appreciation of what each person brings to my life including you, Ray and Richard.

Through this process, I have had the opportunity to make peace with some of my own life decisions. As you pointed out, coming to terms with the fact that a bad decision did not make me a bad person. I've had a chance to feel proud of myself for the work I have done and proud of my family for their support and acceptance. These things have all been so significant and I must say thank you for having the courage to write me once again and thanks to God for giving me the courage to try to face it. He has been so present in this journey and my relationship with Him is at a level I didn't know was possible so I am very grateful.

The process has also had its difficulties. I had to come to terms with my own negative thoughts, beliefs, feelings and actions. I feel like two sides of a coin. Sometimes I feel stuck in one place and other times I feel like I have moved too quickly. Many of my thoughts and feelings have been challenged and I find I have lost some trust in knowing my own feelings.

With each big step I take, I find it only leads to more questions and more feelings and I wonder if there is ever going to be a day where it all feels normal. I often still am stuck in feeling this was never supposed to happen. It was a closed adoption and you were never supposed to know who I was. Sometimes I want to go back to six months ago when none of this was going on and life seemed easier. This has been a lot of hard work. It is in those times I try to focus on the good that has come from this.

I am only just beginning to understand the hurt I experienced 38 years ago. Even pain that was unintentional hurts.

It is overwhelming for me to hear you have thought of me everyday of my life. Sometimes I feel like there is a pressure for me to live up to an expectation of who you think I am. We barely know each other. I know that has been because of my reluctance to open up to you as well as to ask questions about you. I am afraid to open up. I am afraid you will want too much from me. I am afraid you are looking for me to tell you every story from my past. I am so guarded about those things.

This has been hard for all of us and the fact that we are all at different places in this journey makes it all the harder. You have desired this always, Ray and Richard have known about me almost all their lives. You are so far ahead of me. I watch my husband and my children and it just seems easy for them, they don't carry the hurt that I do. That is where I am stuck. I can't seem to let go of the hurt so I can be more open, have more trust, and be more ready. It had been easy over the years to stay closed off from this situation; I could pretend it didn't really affect me. Now I have dealt with it I can see how very much it did affect me and not often for the better.

I can see how much I have changed in these past few months. I went to the first appointment with Jenny and I was so mad and so angry. The problem being I wouldn't admit to it and then once I could admit to it, I wasn't sure why I was angry. I have a better understanding now and can only hope to keep moving forward. The hard part is the future is unknown. I know what happened in the past, it is much easier to stay living there, where thoughts and feelings are familiar. Ultimately, it comes down to this I am scared.

I have every hope the appointment goes well on Wednesday and we both can leave feeling we understand each other a bit more. I'm planning to see you around 11:15 at the McDonald's just to the right of exit 18.—Christine

I worked that morning and then drove to the parking lot. Diane was there. She followed me to Jenny's office. As we waited for the appointment, Diane gave me copies of the letters I had sent to her over the years. I glanced over them quickly and it struck me. My letters to her, her letters to me, they were quite polite and benign. There was no name-calling or character assassinations. Diane's letters to me were full of family stories and her desire to know me. My letters to her were brief notes about current situations. Over 15 years I had written to Diane eight times. If someone read the exchange of letters, I think the person would assume Diane and I had met and had a pleasant and casual relationship.

*   *   *

Jenny called me in first. She asked what I wanted to cover in the session. I said I wanted to talk about the letters Diane had sent to the kids and how out of control it made me feel. I wanted to convey the overall situation still scared me. I went out and asked Diane to come in. Jenny facilitated the conversation asking both of us questions. I couldn't look at Jenny or Diane; I stared at a red book on Jenny's shelf for 90 percent of the session. When we talked about the letters Diane expressed she didn't realize how I would interpret them. Jenny asked me, "How did you feel when the letters came?" I talked about feeling invaded. It snapped me right back to 15 years earlier and how I felt when Diane contacted me the first time. Jenny advised this would probably not be the last time this type of situation would happen. Jenny cautioned me to stop associating this breach on the same level of the first contact. In all actuality, were the letters to the kids equal to my feelings at the time of the original phone call? She had a good point, not that I wanted to admit to it.

Diane removed a stack of papers from her bag. Tearfully she explained they were copies of letters and receipts from all of the years of searching. She told us it had taken four years to get a copy of her own medical records from my birth. She wanted me to understand just how hard she worked to find me. She wanted to convince me she loved me. I was not even sure I wanted to have a relationship with this woman and here she was trying to talk about loving me. My protective reflexes were working overtime. Diane said that she was afraid too. She was fearful she would do or say something that would upset me and I would stop our contact. Jenny worked hard to get us each to see the other person's side of the story. It made me think of our first letters from nearly 15 years earlier. I wrote, "I never wanted to be 'found'. I need you to *accept* that." Diane's letter to me stated, "I read how you never wanted to be found; I will accept that. I have the same desire for your acceptance of the fact that I have *always* wanted and worked toward finding you." I said it was black, she said it was white and in all honesty, it was a weird shade of green.

The session ended and we each thanked Jenny for her help. Once downstairs I asked Diane if she wanted to have lunch. We ran an errand to a hardware store and then went to a restaurant. As we waited for our food, I thanked her for coming to the appointment. I said not everybody would probably open herself up to a stranger as she just had and I was appreciative. She looked at me and said, "I am in it for the long run. I will do whatever it takes." I don't remember all of our discussion but I do remember I made a bit more eye contact and was a little more conversational, not so many one-word answers. I paid for lunch stating Ray and I had an agreement; whoever drove the farthest would not have to pay. She thanked me and we went out to the parking lot. As we said goodbye I thanked her again for coming. As she turned to say goodbye I offered my hand, I could see she was prepared to hug me and her disappointment was evident. We shook hands and went our separate ways.

*   *   *

I spoke to Ray later that night on the phone. He sounded annoyed. I asked if he had talked to his mother. He told me he had and she didn't sound too good. When he talked to Diane, she told him she felt our meeting that day was a step backwards. She was upset and just kept saying she was sorry over and over again. I'm sure my explanation of being hurt, even though she didn't mean to, was weighing on her. I asked if she had mentioned that I didn't hug her; she had. I tried to explain to Ray that hugging was just not that important to me. I told him, "I don't even hug my sister unless it's a holiday, a funeral or the birth of a baby." I said that I express my emotions with other actions. It would have been very easy for me to thank her for coming at Jenny's office and then let her go home. Instead, I went with her to a store and then treated her to lunch. Weeks before, I was talking to a friend and said, "I can only give what I have to give. No more." How much more did Diane want from me?

Ray shared with me some of the hardships he and Richard experienced while growing up. I sensed he was upset that Diane felt she had to apologize to me. I think Ray, Richard and Diane all assumed my life growing up was significantly better than it would have been had Diane kept me. I will be the first to admit my life has been great. I have been fortunate. I have had wonderful experiences and opportunities and I am grateful. My life, however, was not perfect. Nobody has a perfect life. When Ray referred to this I said, "You can't play the what-if game with me." I explained for all they knew, if she had kept me we could have been okay. Maybe if she kept me, she wouldn't have entered into a difficult marriage. Maybe she would never have had another child. Maybe the two of us would have had a lovely life. Who knows?

It was hard for me to clear my mind of all these thoughts. I was not sleeping well. In fact, I was barely sleeping at all. One day I showed up for an appointment with Jenny with the biggest cup of coffee I could find. I don't even really like coffee. When she asked me how much sleep I was getting, I was honest and told her about two to three hours a night. She suggested that maybe it was time to talk with my primary physician about medication. I thought she was talking about sleeping pills. I brushed off the suggestion, asking she give me a couple more weeks. Maybe I could turn it around on my own.

Chapter 5

DISTRACTIONS

The next few weeks continued to be tense. We were all dealing with so much. My 20th high school reunion proved to be a wonderful diversion. During the week leading up to the reunion, I kept saying the only person I cared to see was Mark. He had been a good friend in school but we lost touch after sophomore year of college. Mark was kind and funny and always made you feel like you were his best friend. Everyone in school thought the world of him. Standing in front of the restaurant, I swear I felt the hair on the back of my neck move. I turned around and Mark was walking up the parking lot. We embraced, said our hellos, introduced our spouses and headed inside. That night I saw people who have stayed local as well as people I had not seen since graduation. We visited with our good friends Bonnie, Glen and Cheryl who live out of state.

In addition to Mark, I reconnected with Linda, an old girl scout and field hockey friend. We had seen each other here and there over the years but had not really visited in a long while. I had often thought that Linda and I led parallel lives. She had a sister who was very much like my brother, our mothers were practically the same person and about 10 years before my nephew was born, Linda's nephew was born with Down syndrome. I had been so nervous about going to the reunion but in the end, it had provided me with some much-needed comic relief. I laughed more in that night than I had in weeks. I wrote Mark and Linda notes saying how happy I was to reconnect with them. At the same time, I wondered how I lost touch with two people who previously meant so much to me. I continued to think a great deal about relationships, how they are formed and how they are maintained.

*   *   *

As if I didn't have enough going on that summer, my husband, the kids and I were all in a theatrical production at our church. Our priest had written the play and was interested in putting on the show. It had started when Allison and Cole wanted to do it. Soon enough Kate wanted a part too. Eventually Father Marty called and said he needed Murph and me to take on non-speaking roles. How do you say "no" to a priest? Practices were twice a week usually four to five hours each time. It was a huge commitment. It was the first time all five of us were involved in the same thing. We always supported each other going to games, plays and concerts but this was the first event for all five of us together. It was fun.

I did manage to socialize some through the summer. At a lunch with Mary, I talked about not wanting to share everything with Diane. There were certain pieces of information, which seemed far too personal and confidential to divulge. One might assume I was referring to bank account numbers and dating history. In reality I was completely guarded over the dates of my children's birthdays, types of injuries I had as a child and the biggest one; the fact I had my tonsils out at age eight. (I know, I know, that is why I was still in counseling.) Those pieces of information probably don't seem too private, but to me, they were privileged. The only people who had the right to know those things were my family. Mary continued to be a voice of reason. She asked if holding back the information was a way of punishing Diane. Did I think Diane did not *deserve* to learn those facts about me? Two days later I emailed Diane the following information; my husband's and children's birthdays, our wedding anniversary, the fact I had stitches from a fall when I was seven and finally, the fact I had my tonsils out in 1977.

Murph and I also had dinner with our friends Gary and Jackie. Jackie had heard me over the months and knew how the story progressed. As we ate, I told her a bit more and she commented, "I can remember when the conversation revolved around 'her', 'she' and 'them'. You have opened your mind and that has allowed you to open your heart." All I could picture was the ending to the Grinch when his heart grew three sizes and busted the box surrounding it.

*   *   *

Ray continued to talk about being redeployed. He had no set date but he wanted to go back and was ready whenever the opportunity was presented. I didn't understand his desire to go back to war. He had seen terrible things. He had lost friends and comrades. When I asked Ray about it he told me being a soldier was what he wanted from the time he was a young boy. He attempted to enlist eighteen times in thirteen years. He kept being rejected because of a vision problem. Ultimately, he was allowed to join the Naval Reserves. He then transferred to the Air Force National Guard and served in Iraq for 6 months. Serving in the military seemed to give Ray his drive in life. I didn't want him to lose that, but why couldn't his calling be less dangerous.

Richard continued his studies to be a physician's assistant. With his busy schedule of rotations and the possibility Ray would go overseas, I suggested the three of us spend a weekend together. I wanted to have time with them without Murph, Diane or the kids. I suggested it to Ray and he thought it was a good idea. I sent Richard an email and was happily surprised when he called me later that same day to brainstorm locations. We settled on a camping trip, as it would be less expensive than a hotel. I pictured us sitting around a campfire, having a few beers and talking about all that had transpired over the past few months. We agreed on a date towards the end of August. It would be the weekend following my family vacation at Schroon Lake.

The week I spent at the lake with my husband and children was marvelous. The kids are now old enough where they do not need so much supervision. We went swimming and fishing everyday. More than once I heard myself say, "When Uncle Danny and I were little . . . blah, blah, blah." I told stories of jumping off rope swings into the lake, friends we met each summer and all of our famous camping injuries. While packing for the week I put in several books. I promised myself I was going to read, but no books on adoption or reunions. It would be a week to put all of that aside. I read six books in seven days; I even impressed myself. The night before we came home, I received a call from Richard. His schedule had changed; he would not be available the following weekend but he was off for the next few days. We arrived home on Saturday and several phone calls later, I had a new plan with Ray and Richard. Murph awoke on Sunday to hear I was leaving that afternoon and would be back the following night. He was supportive and even took my car to be serviced before I left.

I drove to Plattsburgh to pick Ray up from the ferry. We then drove to his house to get his gear and eventually made our way to Moose Pond. Richard was in the parking lot when we arrived. I did not ask many questions when we made the plan. They said camping; I assumed that meant campsites, outhouses and picnic tables. You know what they say about making assumptions! Moose Pond is a very unofficial campground. There are no tables and no outhouses, only signs nailed to trees marking off the "safe" areas. We would have to hike in everything that we needed for the overnight stay. We walked 20 minutes on a "trail" (crawling under and over fallen trees) to our "site" (a large opening between trees overlooking the pond 15 feet below). I wasn't sure how to handle Richard's sense of humor. About 18 minutes into our trek, my expression must have been easy to read as I wondered how much further. In reality, it was probably not so much my expression that he read, but the sweat dripping from my face. Richard looked back and stated, "We're about half way there." I tried to hide my shock. The joke was on me when I saw his tent at the clearing only a minute or two later. It was a beautiful view. They pitched my tent and then settled in for "dinner." Ray had a selection of MREs. Being quite naïve I had to ask what an MRE was. It was a military Meal Ready to Eat. Open the package, pour in some water and let the magic begin. I had Salisbury steak. When they asked what I thought, I could answer in all honesty, it was not bad. I had certainly eaten worse. Ray and Richard spent time talking to each other about people they knew and updating town gossip. I just listened. They started telling stories of their military service as well as some daring tales from their teenage years. I just listened. They would go on to tell me a story, one that had never been shared with anyone else. Not friends, not girlfriends, not even Diane had been privy to this adventure. To protect the names of the innocent I will not share it here.

Eventually Richard asked me to tell a story from my life. I said, "Compared to you guys my life has been boring. I have no tales to tell." My life had been straightforward. I went to high school, went to college (they already knew about failing out), got married and had kids. For the rest of the evening we roasted marshmallows and had a couple beers. It was getting cold and the fire was beginning to die out. We all went to bed. I thought about everything as I tried to fall asleep. I had expected we would talk a great deal about our situation, about meeting, about our future. None of that happened. I had packed cards and poker chips in case we needed something to do. Thankfully, we didn't need them; our conversation was enough.

It turned out we were in the coldest place in the United States that night. It even made the news, 30 degrees overnight. In the morning, Richard made us all breakfast, scrambled eggs, home fries and toast. He was obviously a skilled camper as he did this all with a "stove" which was the size of a lantern. Richard asked, "Do you want another piece of toast?" I responded I did and his next statement to Ray was, "Sister wants more toast." I wasn't sure what to say. Didn't he recall our conversation about that subject? As we cleaned up, Richard looked in the cooler. He laughed and said, "We *can't* have this," holding up a few beers. "We can't carry out beer." So, we each enjoyed an after-breakfast beverage, then packed our things and hiked out. In the parking lot, we found someone to take our picture. I only had one exposure left on a disposable camera so we had no idea what it would look like. I hoped it would be nice.

Ray asked if I would be willing to stop at Diane's on my way home. I agreed. Ray rode with me and along the way he asked, "Do you feel you made the right decision in meeting everyone?" I said in the beginning, facing the situation was not really about them. It was about figuring out why it was hard for me. As tough as those initial meetings had been, they were not rough because of them, it was because I still wasn't ready to let go. On the way to Diane's, Ray and Richard insisted we stop at a famous local ice cream stand. In the beginning of this journey, I was concerned about not feeling connected to these two men. We had no common experiences. This overnight trip was indeed a shared event. I commented to friends it felt like a fraternity initiation. It felt like they wanted to see what I could take. Isn't hazing illegal?

We stopped at Diane's for coffee. The four of us sat at the kitchen table as she asked about our evening. They did most of the talking but I did manage to laugh here and there. As I went to leave, Diane offered me a pie she had baked. I looked at it. It was in a glass pie plate and a nice travel container. These things need to be returned I thought. Am I willing to take something that needs to be returned? By taking the pie, am I committing to another visit? (Who says I over think things?) I took the pie. I said my goodbyes and drove home. Over the next two hours as I drove home, I had a lot to consider. The date was August 20, 2007. It was *exactly* 15 years to the day from when Diane called me for the very first time. How weird was that? After everything that had occurred over the past six months, who would have thought I would have been sitting at my birthmother's house with my two half-brothers after a night of camping?

I had the camera developed the next day. The picture came out great.

*   *   *

At the next play practice, one of the other cast members asked why I had missed the last rehearsal. Apparently, my kids had told her I had a "family thing." I said, "It's a long story but here is the short version." I went on to tell her the story as briefly as I could. All of a sudden, I saw tears in her eyes. I stopped. She told me she and her husband had adopted their son. She said her husband was adopted too. I felt I was meant to meet these people. Were they there to teach me or the other way around? Maybe both? Lori would become an amazing resource to me. I could ask her questions about what it was like to be an adoptive mother. These were questions I was afraid to ask my own mother.

Before summer vacation ended, I took my kids to one of those paint-your-own-pottery places. As I looked at the project choices, my eyes stopped at a deviled egg plate. I recalled a story Diane told me. The previous year at Christmas, Ray and Richard surprised her with a trip to Florida. She told me she was touched by their generosity. She was also quite surprised as her request had been for a new deviled egg plate. I decided to make the plate. I felt positive when making it, but when I picked up the finished product a week later, I experienced my typical remorse. Why did I make it? When would I give it to her? What would she think it means? I was always afraid my actions would be interpreted to mean more than I intended.

Not long after making the plate, I had lunch with a colleague. I had known Cathi for about 10 years. Only in the last three or four years did I know she adopted her daughter. In the past few months, I had told her a little bit of the story. Over lunch, I told her about the camping trip, about making the plate and about my hesitation in presenting it to Diane. She encouraged me, telling me to concentrate on the emotions and feelings I had the day I made it. Cathi also continued to help me understand her experience as an adoptive mother. We talked about control. An adoptive family is in control when they sign the application to adopt, they make a conscious decision to proceed. A birthmother is in control when she signs the papers to relinquish, she makes a conscious decision to proceed. The baby does not get a say. The baby does not get to sign anything. The baby has no control. It was becoming clearer and clearer to me why I had issues with control, why I always felt the need to be in charge.

The kids and I met Diane for lunch the day before school started. She was in the area for a medical appointment. I was anxious about a problem with work and it distracted me for much of the meal. The kids seemed to enjoy themselves though and had lots of conversation with Diane. As we went to leave, Diane asked if she could give each of the kids a small gift, some school supply stuff. I hesitated. Would it be okay? What would it mean if I agreed? I nervously allowed the transaction. In turn, I went to my car to get the pie plate and the travel container. I looked at the bag containing the egg plate. I touched it and then let go. I touched it and let go again. I took a deep breath and picked up the bag.

"Here are your things, and I took the kids to a place and I made this. I remembered the story about the egg plate at Christmas." All I could think was, don't think too much of this. It does not mean that I care about you. It does not mean we have a relationship. It does not mean I care about you. I was shaking as she took it from my hand.

"Oh, it is very nice. Thank you."

"Okay. Bye." I walked to the driver's side of the car quickly. I had managed to leave with just a wave.

The next day I had an appointment with Jenny. Due to vacations and tight schedules, I had not seen her in over a month. We first talked about the camping trip with Ray and Richard and seeing Diane on our "anniversary." It was a good conversation; I was excited to share the positive experiences. I then brought up seeing Diane for lunch the day before. I told Jenny about the plate and how hard it had been to give it to Diane. When Jenny asked why, I explained about my fear that Diane would read too much into it. I was afraid she would think I care about her and I am willing to be her friend. (I know; it was a plate . . . not a kidney!) This was one of those moments where, merely saying all of it aloud was enough to help me see the truth. I admitted to Jenny that I understood I was not concerned about *Diane* reading too much into my actions. In truth, I was afraid to let *myself* feel the connection. As I made this admission there sat Jenny, nodding her head because she already knew.

As we discussed this, I admitted part of the issue was still feeling like I was betraying my mother. I didn't know if I would ever get past that. Several of my sentences started, "If only my mother could . . ." Many of these statements had to do with being able to discuss things on an emotional level with my mother. Jenny and I talked a little more and she eventually said, "This has been a central theme for a while. There were things you needed in your life (certain types of support and validation), things your mother didn't provide. Are you afraid Diane may provide some of those things for you?" If I were sitting just a little closer, I may have reached out and hit Jenny. How dare she? How dare she say my mother fell short of perfect? Of course, she was only summarizing things I had been saying for six months, but still, how could she!

During the rest of the day, I came to an important realization. I held my mother in such high esteem; I had put her on such a high pedestal there was no human way for her to live up to my expectations. Why did I do this to her? I finally figured it out. I had put her on that unreachable pedestal because . . . *she saved me*. She took me in when I did not have a home. She took one look at me as that 10-week-old baby, and agreed on the spot, she would forever love me. I had no real name; Diane said she named me Rebecca but on the adoption papers, I was listed as "Mary." Up until that point, I was kind of like a "Jane Doe." My mother was more than an angel; she was practically a god. In the long run, I can see this was not healthy for her or for me.

So let's connect the dots from holding my mother on a pedestal for saving me to being upset with the person who put me in the position of needing saving. I was beginning to see if my life was a building; my mother would live in the penthouse and Diane would live in the basement. Nothing my mother could do would ever let me think less of her and there wasn't anything Diane could do to have me think more of her. Believe me these were not thoughts that made me proud. In fact, I started to think I was a pretty awful person.

*   *   *

I emailed Diane that night trying to explain why something as simple as meeting for lunch and giving her the plate was so hard for me. I wrote about feeling as if I was betraying my mother and the idea I had put her on the pedestal. I talked about having lots of friends who had at one time or another taken on a mothering role in my life. I did not feel any of *them* were a betrayal to the sacred relationship with my mother. It boiled down to this, Diane is *not just somebody else.* I was struggling. I wrote to her that my heart had already accepted so much but there were times my brain would not follow. I had mixed feelings. Diane replied she understood as best she could. Her parents separated when she was in her early twenties. She was close with her mom but there were times when she needed help from her dad for rides and help moving. She fought the idea that asking her dad for help was a betrayal to her mother. She ended by asking me to light a candle. She then wrote to light five other candles off the flame of the first. She wrote the light of the first candle does not diminish just because it lit the other five. Diane asked I see the other five candles as her, Richard, Ray and his family. Showing love and caring toward them would not lessen the love and caring I could show to others.

All of this emotional work was exhausting and I didn't think I could keep going. One day I thought, "This is too hard. I need a break. Maybe I'll *walk away* for a little while. Not from being in contact with Diane, Ray and Richard, but a break from the work of it all. Maybe I would take a break from my appointments with Jenny."

The following Saturday night in church, I had another instance where I truly felt God was guiding my journey. Father Marty was talking about the play. He told us of how he had written it over 10 years ago. He said he wasn't sure he would ever be able to see it as a full production. It had taken the right combination of people at the right time to make it all fall into place. He told us there had been many obstacles in recent weeks, his cat died, he himself became quite ill and a cast member had a death in the family. Many things made him question whether it all would work out. Father Marty told us there were times when conditions were tough, but in the end, the play had turned out to be more successful than he could have ever imagined. He was grateful. At the end of his homily he said, "I encourage you, in whatever you are working on in your own lives. There may be times when it is hard, sometimes you will feel like you want to *walk away*, but don't, keep working, the end result will be better than you can imagine." I started to look around. Was I the only one in church? Had he really just used the phrase "you may want to walk away?" Who is listening to my thoughts? I felt like the whole speech was for me and me alone. I wanted to cry. After the mass, I went to Father Marty and told him what had just happened. He was happy for me. He told me, "I use the words that I feel God wants me to say." Those must have been the words God wanted me to hear. He embraced me as I cried.

This play, the one I had resisted joining, provided so much for my family and me. The five of us bonded as a family over the torturous practices, hours long in the heat of the summer. While none of us had any lines in the play, we laughed when something at home would make one of us think of something a character would say and we promptly recited the line. We connected as a church family with other participants. Many inside jokes were created during the frequent "down time" between scenes. Months later, the jokes still crack us up. I met Lori and her family, a wonderful act of fate.

Chapter 6

AN UNEXPECTED LOSS

I went for an appointment with Jenny and told her about wanting to walk away. I told her how Father's homily seemed directed right at me. I told her I wanted to keep going. I decided it was time to have Diane, Ray and Richard meet my parents, my brother and my sister. They had all been ready for years; I was the one that held back.

I planned a picnic at our house on Sunday, September 30. I planned it right down to who would arrive when. I would ask Ray, Richard and Diane to arrive at 1 p.m. I figured they could see the house and settle in before my family arrived. I would ask my parents and siblings to arrive an hour later. I spoke to Danny on the Monday night before the picnic. I asked him to come over to meet everyone. He said he would come. He sounded down and depressed. He was alone because his girlfriend's brother had died and she was in Chicago with her family. Danny told me the restaurant where he worked was having trouble with the liquor license and needed to shut down. He didn't think it would reopen and he would need to find another job. He sounded all garbled; I thought it was my cell phone. I was in the basement and I thought the reception was sketchy. We were on the phone for about 10 minutes.

Over the next few days, I talked with all the necessary players. Diane, Ray and Richard each told me they were looking forward to the visit. I spoke to my parents and my mother offered to make something. I asked her to bring her world-famous eggplant parmesan. My sister and I exchanged several emails that week. I could be honest with her about my anxieties. I told her I knew it would be weird; there would be no way to act as if it were any other picnic. I confided in Martha I was sure everyone would be fine but I was worried about Danny. I wondered if meeting my biological family would cause him to question why his birthmother hadn't found him. I wrote to her that I was hopeful the love my birth family was giving to me could carry over to Danny. I wanted him to see birthmothers do in fact love their children; Danny's birthmother loved him even if she did not search for him. Martha wrote me back that she thought Danny would be fine. She too was hopeful Danny could find peace in his life and end his cycle of addiction.

*   *   *

During the week, I spoke to many friends saying the get-together was really going to happen; they were all going to meet. I asked Mary to meet me Friday morning before school. I couldn't imagine taking this step without her words of encouragement. I went over to school and we sat at a table near the playground. She asked how I was doing. I admitted I was nervous. Mary pulled from her pocket a note for me. She had written about forgiveness and included a bible quote (something she had done for me frequently on this journey). I was grateful for her time and promised to stay in touch through the weekend. I went on with my workday. Some parents, ones I had known for a long time, knew about the impending meeting. At the very last visit of the day I said, "This is really a big deal. Even my brother is coming over. I don't think he has been at my house in over seven years. This is a really big deal." She wished me luck and I went home.

I decided to try to take it easy that evening. I would have plenty of time to clean and prepare on Saturday and Sunday morning. I sat up in my bed reading for a few hours. I was reading a book on adoption. The chapter I was reading dealt with addiction. I could see my brother in every statement that was written. As I finished the chapter, I thought about Danny. How could I help him? How could I get him to think about all the things I had thought about in these past months? How could I get him to see it was better on the other side of the pain? How could I get him to see it wasn't his fault? I went downstairs to email Mary. I wanted to thank her for the time and the energy she had invested in me. I wrote about my brother and how forgiveness was something I worked for so many times but it had eluded me. I had finally come to realize, I was the one who needed forgiveness. I needed that forgiveness from my harshest critic, myself.

*   *   *

As I typed, the phone rang. It was Ray. We talked of the upcoming meeting and how we were all doing. I shared with him my feelings about Danny. I was worried it would be too emotional for him. My cell phone rang and I had to run upstairs to the kitchen. Who would be calling? It was 11:30 at night. I didn't recognize the number on the caller ID but I answered it anyway.

"Crissy this is Karen." (My brother's girlfriend.)

"Hold on a minute." I switched phones. "Ray, I have to go." I switched phones again. "I'm back."

"Do you know what is going on?"

"No."

"Danny died."

I fell to the floor. Not just to my knees, I literally fell completely over. I began to scream, cry, and pound my fists on the floor. A moment later Murph was standing over me confused. I kept saying it over and over, "Danny died. Danny died. Danny died." I reached for my cell phone to see if Karen was still on the line. She wasn't. I handed the phone to Murph and asked him to call her back. I was still screaming and crying and all I could say was, "Oh my God!" repeatedly.

While Murph was trying to get Karen back on the cell, my home phone rang. The caller ID said Saratoga Hospital. I answered.

"Crissy, its Dad."

"Dad, Dad, Dad," I cried.

"Danny's dead."

"I know. Karen called. How is Mom?"

"She is okay."

"Does Martha know?"

"No."

"Don't call her, I'll go get her. Oh my God. Dad, Dad, Dad."

In that brief moment, I wanted to spare my sister the pain of hearing it on the phone. I hung up with my dad.

I kept saying "Oh my God" over and over. Murph was in with the kids. The screaming woke them up. I told him to get the kids dressed and bring them to the hospital I was going to get Martha. I was in shorts and a sleep shirt so I ran upstairs and grabbed my shoes and a bra. When I came back down, I told Murph he should take the kids to his father's instead and then meet me at the hospital. I called Stacie asking her to drive me to Martha's house. I, at least, had the presence of mind to know I shouldn't try to drive. As I walked across the yard, I called my Aunt Barb in Buffalo. When she answered, I told her Danny died and I didn't know what happened but I would call back soon. I called Ray back and told him what happened. (After everything was said and done, I looked at the call history on my cell phone. In a six-minute span, I got the call from Karen and was out the door to Martha's, having made three phone calls. Adrenaline is an amazing thing.)

Stacie got in the car and asked me what was going on. The only thing she heard me say on the phone was I needed help. She looked stunned when I told her that my brother died and I needed her to drive me to my sister's house. As we drove to Martha's I called Karen back. I didn't even know what had happened. Danny had sounded so depressed on the phone earlier in the week I was concerned he took his own life. She told me he had gone to the ER with chest pains. Mom and Dad were with him and he was being admitted. Karen said that she spoke with Danny around 10 p.m. and that Mom and Dad were going home because a room became available. About a half hour later, she called the hospital to check on his status. A nurse told her that Danny had just died. She knew that my parents had been called to come back to the hospital but had not yet arrived. That is when she called me.

Stacie and I got to Martha's house. It was about midnight. I walked across the gravel driveway in my bare feet. The pain of the rocks on my skin was dull in comparison to the ache in my heart. I started knocking on the door and ringing the doorbell. No answer. I knocked on my 3-year-old niece's window. I could see her stirring. "Go get Mommy. It's Aunt Crissy, go get Mommy." She did not wake up.

I called the house with my cell phone, no answer. I yelled into the machine "Martha, its Crissy, come open the door! Martha! Come open the door!" No response. I called three times. Nothing. The whole time I was calling, I kept knocking on the door and ringing the doorbell, still no response. I looked at Stacie and laughed, "You've got to be f***ing kidding me!" We stood out front for over five minutes to no avail. I walked around the back of the house and surprisingly the sliding glass door was not locked. I opened it, went in, turned on lights and then opened the front door for Stacie. I walked down the hall and opened the bedroom door. My sister and her husband were fast asleep; they had heard nothing. I stood over my sister jostling her leg. She opened her eyes a little.

"Martha you need to get up. Danny died. We need to go. Danny died!" She sat up a little and then laid back down closing her eyes. Perhaps she thought she was dreaming. Martin opened his eyes and I repeated everything. I started crying really hard. Martha woke up more and it started to sink in. It was the absolute worst moment of my life. I had tried to protect Martha for so many years. There was no protection from this. Martha and

Martin got out of bed. I went back to the kitchen and leaned against the table. I started sobbing. I fell to my knees and eventually fell all the way onto the floor. I was crying so hard. I had no idea anything in life could hurt this much. Stacie put her hand on my back as I wept.

Martin made calls to have someone stay with their kids. I told Martha I wanted to get to the hospital to be with Mom. I was so worried about Mom. I offered for her to come with Stacie and me. She wanted to wait and go with Martin. I hugged Martha and Martin then left. Stacie drove me to the hospital. I called on our way over and asked to talk to Dad. He told me Mom was doing okay. I told him I was on the way and Martha would be there soon. The 20-minute drive was more than I could take. I felt like a pendulum, vacillating between uncontrollable sobbing and stoic disbelief.

*   *   *

We arrived at the hospital and I put on my shoes and my bra. Stacie held on to me as we entered the hospital. It was like an out-of-body experience. I didn't feel my feet below me. I think the nurse could tell exactly who I was. She directed me to the room without even asking why I was there. I started to walk into the wrong room and Stacie held my arm tight as she helped me. The door opened and there he was. My mom was sitting beside him and my dad was standing by his head. There was still a tube taped in his mouth. "Mom, Mom, Mom". It felt like I said it hundreds of times. I hugged her.

"It is okay. You made your peace with him. It is okay." I don't know exactly how I felt but I knew "okay" was not the word I would have used.

Stacie hugged my mom, kissed my cheek and told me to call if I needed her. In the days that followed, I could not find sufficient words to thank Stacie for all she had done.

Mom kept telling me she was okay. Dad was stroking Danny's hair. I moved to the other side of Danny, held his hand and silently said a Hail Mary. Mom looked at me and said, "He said he was Catholic." I didn't understand what had happened. She explained when Danny was being admitted, the nurse asked if he wanted a religion noted on the bracelet. She told him Methodist was what was on file for him. Mom said Danny looked at the nurse and asked her to change it to Catholic. My mother was sitting right beside Danny as that happened. I thought about it a great deal in the days that followed. I believe Danny was asking for salvation. Whether he knew he was going to die, I don't know. I do think, however, God was touching his life that night.

A few minutes later Murph arrived. He told me the kids were okay with his dad. He hugged my parents and me. Martha and Martin arrived. It was this unreal moment. The six of us stood there around the bed, each of us staring and trying to believe he had really died. Martha leaned into me, "I don't care if anything else ever comes of you meeting your biological family; at least it brought you and Danny back together." First Mom's comment and now Martha's, I was beginning to realize just how much my rift with Danny affected the rest of the family. I felt selfish and guilty.

I went outside and called Mary. It was almost 1 a.m., but I needed to talk to her. I kept apologizing that it was so late but I had to talk to her. I told her Danny died and all I could hear in my head was her voice, "If you knew it was all going to be over, would you rush to get there?" She listened as I cried and sobbed about all that had just happened. I don't remember all I said, but I can hear myself telling her, "You were so right Mary; you were so right about everything."

When I went back into the room, a nurse came in to tell us there would need to be an autopsy because of Danny's young age. She started to tell us what happened. You hear the exact speech on television shows. She said he was stable, he was on a portable monitor getting ready to transfer to a room and she left to get his paperwork. When she returned two minutes later, he was in a grand mal seizure and arrhythmia. They started CPR, gave numerous medicines, put a tube in and shocked him seven times. Just like on television, she ended with, "Despite all our efforts, we were not able to save him." She kept shaking her head saying they just didn't know what went wrong. There started to be discussions of funeral homes and arrangements. I asked Murph to make the call.

My parents decided to go home. Martha, Martin, Murph and I made plans of what to do next. The four of us stood there for a few minutes. Then Murph and Martin left each saying a final goodbye to our brother. Martha and I stood at Danny's side. We hugged and cried. We kissed each other and then kissed Danny. As we left the room, the nurse looked at us and said, "You girls be strong for your Mom and Dad, they are going to need you." I really wanted to say, "Screw you!!" My brother just died and now you are telling me to be strong for someone else. I wanted to tell her I had spent a lifetime pushing my true feelings aside and would not do that now. I would be sad and devastated and I would not push it aside. Instead of telling the nurse where she could stick her advice, I walked away. (Days later, Martha and I would discover the day of the picnic back in June, three months before his death, was the last day either of us saw Danny alive.)

Murph and I spent the night at his father's house since the kids were asleep when we arrived. We got there at 2 a.m. and I can remember staring at the clock, watching the time tick by. The last I remember, it was about 5 a.m. I slept for about and hour and then waited for everyone else to wake up.

*   *   *

Around seven in the morning, I called Carolyn. At eight, I called Jenny. I don't remember much about either call. The kids woke up around 8:30 and we talked about everything. They sat on the couch with me and I asked if they understood what had happened. Katie asked if Danny was okay. I told them that he died at the hospital, that the doctors and nurses worked hard to save him but his heart was just too weak. They all seemed in shock, not really showing any emotions. Allison was concerned about everyone else. How was I doing? How were Gramma and Papa? The apple didn't fall very far after all. We decided to take them to see my parents and then Murph would take them home. They handled everything amazingly well. Unfortunately, this was not their first experience with death. Three years earlier my mother-in-law, her sister and their mother all died in a six-week span. My kids knew a thing or two about death. My mother was afraid to see the kids. She worried that her immense sadness would scare them. I told her they needed to see it. They were sad too and if they didn't see her being upset, they would be confused. She did not need to put on a happy face. They only stayed a few minutes and then Murph took them home. I know he wanted me to go with him; he wanted to take care of me. I needed to stay with my parents; I needed to take care of them.

After he left, I started going to the neighbors. These were all people who knew my family for over 40 years. Both cars were in the driveway next door but nobody was answering. I was having déjà vu from the night before at Martha's place. I called and left three messages on their machine. I walked across the street; again no answer. Was this some kind of cruel joke? Finally, I spoke to two neighbors. The person from the second house, my "Aunt" Barb (not my real aunt but that is what I called her all my life) yelled out the door to me. Her hair was all wet and she was wrapped in a towel. When I went into her house, she asked what was wrong. All I could say was, "It's Danny." She kept asking what was wrong. I started to cry and repeated, "It's Danny." She finally understood and I saw her knees buckle. I stood up and helped her sit down. A couple minutes later, I went back to my parents' house. My dad was on the phone with his sister. It was devastating to watch.

I started calling my mom's brothers and sisters. My mom couldn't even speak when I tried to give her the phone. Watching her in those first few hours, I saw her cycle through four distinct states of being. She was crying uncontrollably, sleeping, telling weird stories about my brother or sitting dazed on the couch. My father just paced and stayed quiet. I kept making calls to friends and family.

My mother called me into her room. She asked me to find Father Bondi. I asked if she wanted to talk to any priest or specifically Father Bondi. She answered she wanted to talk to Father Bondi. He was the priest of our church for my whole growing-up life. He baptized me and married me. He had retired about ten years earlier and was currently 80-odd years old. He lived in Florida but visited the area in the summer. I began making calls to track him down. My cell phone rang and it was Diane. She told me she was very sorry for our loss and asked how we were all doing. I thanked her for calling but told her I would have to call her back later; I was trying to find the priest.

My sister arrived and we talked to our parents about the arrangements. Neither of them wanted to go to the funeral home. We wrote our brother's obituary. In addition to his survivors, we wrote about his life: Dan will always be remembered for his love of the outdoors, camping trips to Schroon Lake, his passion for cooking, his wry sense of humor and his big brown eyes. The last comment was a specific request from Mom.

Since I had not gone home, I was still in my shorts and nightshirt. Luckily, Martha was able to stop by my house and pick up a change of clothes so I could freshen up. In the shower, I kept turning the handle to make the water hotter and hotter. The intense pain on my skin was beginning to overshadow the pain in my heart. All I could think was, "Now I understand cutting."

Martha and I went to the funeral home and made the plans. After, we went to the church and asked the priest to mention Danny's name during the intentions of the weekend masses. The florist was the next stop. Martha was concerned the flowers look masculine, nothing pink. We went to the grocery store and got some essentials. We knew there would be people in and out of the house for the days to come. It amazed me how we just did these errands as if we were professional funeral planners. We were not given a checklist of things to do; we just seemed instinctively to know what to do.

Back at the house, my brother's girlfriend and her family were all there. I wanted them to go home. I wanted my parents to myself. I felt bad for her, but my main concern was for my parents and I did not want anyone else around.

*   *   *

In the afternoon, Father Bondi called to speak with my mother. She got on the phone and her words were unintelligible. I took the phone from her. I explained what I could. My brother had died. He led a tough life, he walked away from the church several years ago and my mother was concerned about his soul going to heaven. I told him how Danny had told the nurse he was Catholic when he was admitted. Father Bondi assured me Danny was in the kingdom of heaven. I then had to laugh when Father said, "He is in heaven which is where I want to be. I am 86 years old. Yet God leaves me here." I told my mother Father Bondi was positive Danny was in heaven. She took the phone back from me. What happened next is a sight I will never forget. A transformation happened right in front of my eyes. My mother went from an unintelligible, curled up ball of raw nerves to a coherent person who sat up straight. I was witness to the peace of God and all its power. For so many years, my mother did not rest. She was always afraid of something happening to Danny. She was fearful he would leave and she would not know where he was. My mother could now rest. Danny did leave, but we knew where he was, in heaven. God Bless Father Bondi. My prayerful appreciation for the priest was interrupted when I heard my mother's next statement. "Father, do you know me? I am the one with the adopted children. You have helped me so much and now my daughter has met her real mother." Enough was enough; I took the phone from my mother's hand and thanked Father profusely for getting in touch.

The rest of the day was much of the same, phone calls and relaying information about the services. Murph kept calling to check on me. I felt like I was on autopilot. Had it really happened? Was Danny really gone?

I noticed Annette's car across the street in her mother's driveway. Annette was a year older than Danny and was like an older sister while I was growing up. I walked over to the house. Standing in the threshold between the living room and the kitchen Annette put her arms around me. I fell apart. She could understand my pain. She too had witnessed Danny's painful transformation from normal neighborhood kid to troubled youth. She would remember with me that there had been better times in his life. I told her I didn't feel like myself. I felt like I was 10 and I was grieving the loss of my 12-year-old brother. Perhaps that had been the last time we truly had a close relationship. Annette's mother, "Aunt" Barb, kicked her Italian-mother gene into high gear. She was at my side every three minutes offering a different thing to eat. I finally agreed to some chicken noodle soup. I had to laugh when she returned with broth and vegetables telling me she forgot she used all the chicken the day before. Two minutes after that, she returned with a piece of cold pizza telling me it was from the "good place" down the street. I pulled myself back together and went across to see my parents.

As I sat on the couch with my mother she turned and said, "How is your mother, does she know?" I chose not to give my usual expression and sigh when she referred to Diane as "my mother." I simply told her they all knew what had happened. Ray, Richard and Diane each had called to express their sympathy. Her next statement seemed unreal, "You have to tell them to come." I pretended she didn't say it and changed the subject to something else.

*   *   *

I eventually went home that night. I knew my aunt and my cousin were on their way. I knew I could trust them to take care of my mom allowing me to get other arrangements underway. I spoke with Mary. I told her what my mother said about inviting my birth family. She asked what I thought. I eventually told her maybe this is just the way it is supposed to be. I spoke with Ray and Richard briefly telling them what was going on. In my mind I could picture them being at the services. They would be in the back of the church in an anonymous fashion. I would know they were there, I would feel their support but I wouldn't be introducing them to everyone. Richard called and like Diane and Ray, offered to do whatever would be helpful.

I arrived at my parents' on Sunday to find they had gone to church. I was amazed. The strength it must have taken to sit there, hearing my brother's name during the intentions, having people hear of his death for the first time, as they were only a few feet away. My mother later told me she was fine until communion. When she walked up, the Eucharistic minister was my brother's former Boy Scout leader. It was then she fell apart.

I went over to see Annette again. She was baking. She asked, "What is it about death that immediately forces you to bake?" I laughed as I said, "Because it is easier to walk into someone's house and say, 'I made these apple squares for you' instead of 'I am so sorry your person died'."

Back at the house, my father asked me to get some hotel rooms for people coming from out of town. I suggested a bed and breakfast close by. As we talked in the basement I looked him in the eye and said, "Dad today was supposed to be significant for such a different reason." He looked puzzled. I reminded him we were supposed to have the picnic at my house. He apologized for forgetting. I told him what my mother said about inviting my birth family to the service. I told him I was uncertain. He looked me and said, "They are your family, which makes them our family, and they should be with us at this difficult time." Our talk was interrupted by my cell phone. It was Rana; she was just back from a trip and heard all my messages on her machine and cell. I told her what was going on and how I was so confused. She encouraged me and told me it would be okay.

Back in the house, Dad asked me if I had made the phone calls. I asked, "To the bed an breakfast?" He said, "No, the other calls." I knew he was referring to Ray, Richard and Diane. I told him no but I would. He gave me a stern look that told me, "Don't you dare not obey what I've asked you to do."

I went home and called Ray and Richard. I asked Ray to call Diane; I just couldn't talk to her. I told them my parents were adamant they attend the services. Ray and Diane made plans to arrive Tuesday morning for the funeral. Richard was starting a new rotation that day. He tried to explain the situation to his administrator. Unfortunately, there was not a policy to miss a day for your newly found sister's brother's funeral. I understood.

The next morning I went to my parents'. I wished I could just move in there but I also had my family to consider. Murph and the kids were allowing me a lot of freedom and I appreciated it so much. I went with my father to the bank to get a check for the funeral home. He stood by the teller for a minute trying to explain and eventually gestured to me and said, "Just do what she says." When I came out with the check, he asked me to take it up later. I asked why we weren't going now. He didn't say anything. I guessed he did not want to be at the funeral home one more minute than absolutely necessary.

We also went to the grocery store. As we were driving, I told him the church organist waived her normal fee when she learned it was Danny. He told me he was so touched by the outpouring of care and concern. He said, "When this is over we will write each person a thank you note. And we will not mail them; we will deliver each one in person." He asked me about the bed and breakfast. He asked how he should address my birthmother and her sons. I said calling them by first names would be fine. He asked where they were staying. I said they were only coming to the funeral; they did not need rooms. He insisted they come that night for the wake and instructed me to call them and tell them immediately. He said, "They will come to the services, they will join us at the reception and afterward they will come here to the house." I called Ray. I told him what my father said and that my father would pay for their rooms. He called Diane and then called me back. He said they would get packed and leave in a couple of hours. He stated they were uncomfortable with the idea of my dad paying for the rooms. I told Ray I didn't have the energy to argue about it. "If you care at all about me, you will just come. Don't cause more stress by disagreeing about the rooms." He said he understood and would call when they arrived.

I needed to go home and get ready for the wake. On the way, Richard called. I told him Ray and Diane were on their way down to attend the services that evening. He told me he would get in his car and drive over for the wake. I didn't have the strength to oppose. He would be driving for over three hours to see us for a short period of time and then driving right back home. He was probably looking at seven hours of driving in all. I was touched by his desire to support my family and me.

*   *   *

Once home we all got dressed and drove to the funeral home. We took two cars so Murph could leave with the kids if needed. My sister and Martin arrived at the same time we did. Danny's current girlfriend and his two ex-wives were inside. It was quite the sight seeing the three of them standing together, looking over the casket. Martha and I inappropriately wondered if his high school girlfriend would also attend. Later in the evening, we would give each other a knowing wink as the former girlfriend greeted us in line. Danny was never without a woman in his life, I don't think he ever felt comfortable being alone. I questioned if this fear clouded his judgment with matters of the heart. Danny didn't do much dating. He would meet someone and the next thing we knew they were living together or getting married. He did not seem to know how to get to know someone slowly; it was all or nothing.

Martha and I waited for the women to move out of the room before we went in. Seeing Danny was so hard. He looked so old. Where was the brother of my youth? Cole didn't want to go in. A few minutes later, my parents arrived. As they knelt in front of my brother, my father began to sob. I knew there was nothing I could do for him. He got up and went outside trying to collect himself. His sister went out to be with him. My mother went out to the front room and sat with Cole, he cried. The priest came and started a short prayer service. A line of people formed quickly. It was surreal. Friends, family and neighbors came to offer condolences and pay their respects. Mom and Dad were doing amazingly well, taking time to hug each person. I was good until I hugged Martha's father-in-law. Lee has that grandpa look, a lot like a skinny Santa. Something about his embrace made me break down. We introduced ourselves over and over again to those we didn't know. We saw people we had not seen in many years. One time as I looked down the line, I saw Nancy and her father Ron. They were neighbors from our youth. Nancy was my best friend for the first 10-plus years of my life. We played together everyday. I left my place in the line to go to her. As we hugged, I told her how much it meant to see her; she could remember my brother in his better days. She could understand my loss.

Murph kept checking in with me. I was doing okay. Not long after, he told me he saw Stacie, Sean, Mary, Rana and Kaile further down the line. I was anxious to see these friends. Just then, Allison came up to me and told me Diane and Ray were there. I looked and they were right there in front of my friends. I stepped next to my Dad and introduced Diane. He gave her a big embrace and smiled. He shook Ray's hand and thanked them for coming. My mother was talking to someone else; I put my hand on her shoulder. She didn't stop talking. I eventually interrupted her and told her it was important. I held her by the arm.

"This is Diane." My mother took Diane by both shoulders and looked at her. Then she looked at me confused as if to say—tell me who this is. "This is Diane." No recognition. "This is Diane." No recognition. My father, God love him, eventually said, "Diane . . . her birthmother!" I thought I would pass out. Mom's eyes changed, she locked eyes with Diane. It was as if they looked into each other's souls. They embraced and said things I could not hear. My friends had me by the arms at this point. They kept encouraging me to sit down. Murph went to get me a drink. I can only imagine what I looked like. I introduced Diane to my sister. My dad started introducing Diane and Ray to all of our relatives. Most of them had no idea what was going on. I eventually said, "Dad there are a lot of people waiting to talk to you, there is time for this later." He then pointed to two chairs right behind me and asked Ray and Diane to sit down. As I greeted the next people in line all I could feel was their presence behind me. I told them perhaps they would be more comfortable in the other room. I think they were relieved as well and moved to the front room.

A short while later Allison came over to tell me that Richard had arrived. I brought him to the front of the line and introduced him to my parents and sister. Ray came up right after and said Stacie and Sean had offered to take them all to dinner. I told him I would call when things were done.

The line of people kept coming; not a single break in two hours. Around 8:30, Linda, my old Girl Scout and field hockey friend arrived. With the loss of my brother, we truly did lead parallel lives. She lost her brother Jimmy 20 years earlier. The crowd lessened and I actually had a few minutes to visit with her. I felt bad earlier in the evening when it was so busy I barely had more than a minute with each person. Seeing Linda and having time to talk with her was a gift.

Soon it was after 9 p.m. and it was mostly immediate family still hanging around. I suggested if people still wanted to visit, they should go up to my parents' house; otherwise, we would see them in the morning. Linda stood for a long time with me outside the funeral home. Ray called to say they were on their way back from dinner. I asked Linda to go to the bed and breakfast with me and wait for them.

On the way, I checked the messages on my cell phone. Mary had called after leaving the wake. Her voice sounded exhausted and solemn but her words were powerful. "I had a thought Christine. What if this was the plan all along? God knows everyone's plans so he knew when Dan was gonna die, maybe that is why Diane, Ray and Richard came into your life when they did. Maybe that was God's plan. That since you had to lose one brother you gained Richard and Ray, not to replace, but to give to you so that you would not be without. Maybe that was the plan all along. Maybe that is why the timing was what it was tonight? I don't know, just a thought. Love ya, hope everything is alright." (I saved the message and listened to it on a regular basis for over six months.)

Linda and I sat on a bench outside the bed and breakfast. I don't remember what we said. I was tired and I'm sure she was too. It was well after 10 p.m. when they arrived. I introduced everyone and said goodbye to Linda. I went up to Diane's room with the three of them and sat down. They asked how I was doing. I didn't really know how to respond; exhausted and raw didn't seem to do it justice. Richard looked at me and said, "I can't begin to know what you are going through. I know Ray and I don't always get along but I don't know what I would do if I lost him." Ray seemed as touched by the comment as I was. We visited only a few more minutes and then I offered to take Richard back to his car and have him follow me to the highway. He would have a long drive home and an early shift the next day. It meant a great deal to me that he made the trip.

*   *   *

On the way home, I called Rana. I knew it was late . . . but I was sure she would be awake. I needed to hear from someone what it was like . . . what was it like to witness Diane and my mother meeting for the first time. I wasn't sure I could even picture it in my own head. She told me, "It was unreal to see Ray and Diane right in front of us in line. I recognized them from your pictures. I kept trying to tell Mary. I tried to whisper and she didn't hear me. I tried to say it two or three times and Mary kept saying, 'What?' I eventually was able to say, 'Diane is right in front of us.' We kept looking for you to notice that she and Ray were there. When you finally saw her, you looked dazed. Your dad hugged her and then when you tried to tell your mom, it was so obvious she wasn't processing it. We were so worried about you. You looked like you were going to pass out. Murph took good care of you. It was only a few minutes, but it felt longer." We finished talking right as I pulled in the driveway. Some relatives arrived right behind me to spend the night. I helped them settle in Cole's room.

I went downstairs to write a eulogy for Danny. With very few revisions, this is what I wrote.

> *For quite a few years before Martha came along, it was just the two of us. Together with the neighborhood kids, there was hour upon hour of bike riding, skateboarding, kick ball, hide and seek, spud and pickle. We spent the summers camping, fishing and water skiing. He was older,*

bigger and stronger and there was a time when he knew everything there was to know.

Danny was a part of many "firsts" for me. He was with me on my first day of school, the first time I water-skied and as we got older, I'm sure one of his friends was probably my first real crush. But as I think back on our time together, the most important was that he was my first friend.

Like many relationships, ours was not without its ups and downs. Over these past months, we had rediscovered our connection and Danny once again took that role of older, bigger and stronger as he showed me how to live with an open heart. In June, he hosted the entire family for a picnic. Danny and I spoke that day of our lives and how lucky we both were. He told me that he finally felt that he had all that he needed, a woman that loved him, a job that fulfilled him and a home that he was proud of. He once again showed that he knew everything there was to know.

As a family, we are devastated at his loss, but our faith tells us that he is in a better place. When I think of heaven I think of a place that allows you to feel nothing but love and allows you to spend eternity doing only things that bring you happiness. So I am imagining that Danny's heaven is a huge lake for waterskiing that always "looks like glass", a mountain for snow skiing always full of fresh snow, a kitchen full of hungry people to feed and a big porch where friends and family sit and visit, I think these are the things that would bring him happiness.

The experience of the past few days and in particular last night will forever stay with me. To see such a huge outpouring of love was amazing. I am grateful to each and every one of you who offered our family words of support and encouragement.

Losing Danny is that ultimate wake-up call. Life is indeed too short. So even in his death, he is that older, bigger and stronger brother teaching me about life. Teaching me that it is okay to let go of the past, to let go of things that hold me back and to only hold onto love and peace. There were so many times in the past that we feared losing Danny but he always seemed to hang on. I think that when peace and love finally came to him from all the people he cared about, it was time for him to let go. Perhaps once again he knew everything there was to know.

I would be remiss if I did not mention one other fact about Danny, he was a Bills fan. When they won, Danny would not necessarily brag about them winning but would state, "Well at least they didn't blow it again." Sunday's game was a close one but the Bills did win, perhaps with a little influence from above.

I printed it and went to bed.

*   *   *

In the morning, we woke up, had breakfast and got dressed. We drove to the funeral home. On the way there, I cried. Not the sobbing cries of the past few days, but a sad cry where the tears simply would not stop streaming down my face.

Once seated inside, the director led us in a prayer and then called people up in groups to offer a last respect to Danny. When Murph, the kids and I went up, I tried to hold it together. No use, I sobbed as we walked away. I wanted to stay inside and guard over my parents, as they would be the last people to go, but I knew I had to let them have their moment alone and went out to the car.

We drove to the church and waited for everything to be ready. We started walking up the aisle behind the casket. My heart was breaking. I didn't realize that this moment, following his casket into church, would be more difficult than seeing him in the hospital. I wasn't sure I could walk. I grabbed onto each pew as we made our way. I made eye contact with Dawn. I didn't even know she had heard the news. She was a teacher I had been close with in high school. She was the person who received the call from the dean so many years before when Diane was searching for me. Ironically, she was seated right behind Diane and Ray. We made our way to the front and the mass began. I tried to listen to what the priest was saying. I *wanted* to be comforted by his words. After communion, it was time for my brother's son, my sister and me to go up and speak about Danny. I went last. I was shaking so hard I had to hold onto the podium to try to stop trembling. I could get my arms to be still and then my legs would start. I held onto my leg as I spoke. My voice sounded unsteady and I just hoped people could hear what I was saying. We finished and returned to our seats.

The service ended. We would not be going to a cemetery, so the funeral director lined us up outside the church in a receiving line of sorts.

Dawn came up to me and said, "That was so well written (the eulogy), you must have had a wonderful English teacher." We laughed of course, as *she* had been my freshman English teacher. I tried to tell her about Ray and Diane. When I told her she said she knew it immediately; Diane's eyes and hands were the same as mine. Dawn told me she could not stay for the breakfast, but promised to be in touch soon. I spoke to others as best I could. Then I started to hear my father's voice. "Dave, have you met Diane? She is Crissy's mother. This is Ray, Crissy's brother." That familiar queasy feeling washed over me. Was he really doing this? Was he really standing outside the church, immediately following Danny's funeral, introducing everyone, telling them Diane was "my mother"? He did it about 15 more times. Most of these people had no idea I had been in contact with Diane. I could only imagine how confused they were.

We left the front of the church to go to a restaurant for a reception. Once we got there, I stood out front with Ray and Diane for a moment before going in. When we entered, I quickly assessed that the only seats left were at a table with my parents. Our table of eight consisted of my parents, Diane, Ray, Katie, my dad's sister, her friend and me. Each time people came up to the table to see my parents, my dad would again state, "This is Crissy's mother Diane and her brother, Ray." Some people looked stunned; others took a minute to process and then would go, "Ohhh" as they realized the situation. One neighbor, my "Aunt" Diane (another person who was not my real aunt but I had called her that all my life), knelt down to talk with Diane. I only heard a bit but I think she was trying to convey I was a good person, my parents were good people and I had had a really good life.

We started to say our goodbyes. Several people from out of town needed to go back home and would not be going over to my parents. It was hard to let them all go. Many had been our source of support and comfort for the past few days. We were most appreciative of the comic relief they provided. My mother's brothers and sisters told story after story of their childhood. These stories always made my mother laugh and I was so grateful to hear that sound.

Murph, the kids and I were not ready when everyone else wanted to leave so my father instructed Ray and Diane to follow them back to the house. I stood there in the parking lot and watched as they pulled away. I remembered a comment I had made several times when I first considered having everyone meet. I said I should plan something where everyone could meet; I just wouldn't go. They were all clearly ready for it to happen, even when I couldn't fathom it. I was busy in the days following my brother's death. I was not able to stand there and control it all, as I would have liked. I had to let go. Overall, other than the fact my brother died, it went pretty well.

We drove over to my parents' and as I walked into the house, they were all in the living room. My dad was explaining all the pictures on the walls. I walked right through excusing myself to go change. I called and left a message for Jenny praying she would be able to call me back, soon. I walked back out and felt awkward about where I should sit. I pulled a chair up next to my mom. The conversation was casual. We talked about the Adirondacks, camping and fishing. I told how Dad frequently lost his pipe on camping trips. Diane made a comment about losing her wallet and often getting calls from the grocery store saying she had left it in the cart . . . again. My mother smiled and laughed. I knew exactly what she was going to say. She quipped at Diane, "Don't you carry a purse?" She replied no and my mother slapped at my leg. My mother has been trying to teach me to carry a purse for the past 35 years.

Luckily, the phone rang and I left the room. It was Jenny. "They are here. Ray and Diane are here at my parents' house. They are out in the other room. They are all talking to each other. I don't know if I can breathe." She reassured me. When I walked back out into the living room Ray and Diane were saying goodbye to my parents. They had left home on short notice and needed to get back. My mother said, "The next time you are down we'll get out all the albums and show you her pictures." Diane replied she would like that. My mother gestured to me and said, "What was that thing you got from President Reagan?" I tried to shoo off the question saying it wasn't important. (It was a mass-produced post card congratulating me on earning my Girl Scout gold award. I received it in 1986 and it was still framed on the shelf in my old room.) My father looked at me and said, "She is very modest. She is not going to tell you things. But we'll tell everything and she'll just have to trudge along." Then Ray and Diane left.

It was time for us to go too. Murph gathered the kids and we said goodbye to my parents. It was a long few days but we had all survived. I was grateful. Trying to sleep that night, I thought about all that had happened. I looked at the role of God in my life. Each member of our family was touched by God on the night Danny died. Danny had proclaimed he was a Catholic. Mom had been there to witness it. Dad commented, "All the times we left him in the hospital, I always worried because he looked so bad. I didn't worry on Friday night. He really looked okay, he looked good." I told my Dad I felt God was taking care of him, allowing him to have peace about letting Danny go. For my sister, she told a story of preparation. She was due to go to a wedding on Saturday. She purchased new stockings, a new skirt and new shoes. Friday afternoon she ironed everything and put it out for the next day. She told me God had prepared her, not for a wedding, but a funeral. As for me, in the three hours before my brother's death I was completely fixated on him. I prayerfully expressed my desire to help him and my concern for his emotional well-being. In the days after, I would tell friends my faith in God was strengthened a million times over.

*   *   *

I saw Jenny four times in an eight-day span following my brother's death. I wasn't going back to work right away so it seemed to make sense to take advantage of my unexpected flexibility. During the first session, I found it difficult even to say Danny's name. I talked about the events the night he died, about reading the book, sending the email to Mary and talking to Ray. I don't recall giving Jenny an opportunity to say much. Sitting in her office, I received a phone call from the funeral home. Danny's ashes were ready along with a cross we had ordered for my mother. The small silver cross contained a portion of the ashes. Martha and I had agreed one of us would pick up the ashes, but the day before, while speaking to Karen, Danny's girlfriend, she asked to pick them up. I didn't feel like I could say no. She lived with him and they planned to get married. I was only recently reconciled with him; I didn't feel like I could pull rank as his sister. I told her she could pick them up. According to Karen, he wanted them scattered in Schroon Lake.

I drove to the funeral home and took the cross. I called my sister's cell phone and she was at my parents' house. I asked her to wait there so we could give it to Mom together. I walked into the kitchen and saw Dad making some lunch. I told him I had the cross. His face lost its expression. My sister and I presented the cross to our mother. She fought back the tears as she looked at it. Then we laughed because her next statement was, "It is so small; where did they put him?" My mother questioned why Martha and I did not get crosses as well. We both told her we didn't want one. I told her the only things I wanted were a copy of a photo over the fireplace (Danny was 11 and I was 8) and the portrait sketch Danny and I purchased for Mom when we visited Disney in 1978. Mom immediately went to take the frames off the wall. I stopped her saying I didn't mean I wanted them *that minute*. She looked at Martha and me and told us to take whatever we wanted. My sister picked up the phone and stuffed it in her coat pocket making us all laugh.

*   *   *

On Saturday, eight days after Danny died, the whole family went to a christening. "Uncle" Roy and his wife were new parents to a baby girl and I was the godmother. I felt in control of my emotions until Annemarie handed me the baby. I cradled her in my arms as the priest poured holy water over her head. As he blessed her life, I thought of my brother and my own children. I prayed that I would never again have to see a parent outlive a child.

Later that day, I received a thank-you card from my parents in the mail. (Hey, what about my father's promise to hand-deliver all the thank-you notes?) My mother knows me too well. Inside the card she wrote, "Be easy on yourself," underlined three times, "and enjoy life with the red heads." Mom frequently referred to my husband and kids collectively as "the red heads." Dad wrote, "You are very dear to me and I love you deeply." I can only imagine what it was like for them to write the card, to express thanks to one child for helping after the death of another.

*   *   *

On Monday, I went back to Jenny. I talked about my mother and Diane meeting for the first time. I said I felt at peace with Danny's death and my relationship with him. When Jenny asked if I felt at peace with Diane, I said "No."

I saw Jenny again on Tuesday. She asked why it was still so hard with Diane. I told her I knew hurt and anger were still with me. Jenny wanted to know what it would take for me to get past the hurt and the anger. I talked about how difficult it was for me to make eye contact with Diane. I told Jenny I was afraid. I was afraid if I allowed Diane to look into my eyes she would see right into my soul. I could not imagine sharing that much of myself with Diane. She did not deserve to have full access to me. Jenny suggested I try to be aware of my eye contact when I am with Diane, try to have it more often and try to hold it a little longer; this sounded good in theory.

I called Diane that night. Phone calls erased the whole possibility of eye contact. We spoke for three hours. After asking how we were all doing, Diane said she wanted to tell me something. She, Ray and Richard had been planning to go on a cruise for several years. She would soon have access to some retirement money and she wanted to invite Murph, the kids and me to go along on the voyage. She offered to pay for us to join them. I told her it was a generous offer but I couldn't even really think about something as big as a vacation cruise at the time.

We started talking about Danny. Diane wanted to know if Danny and I frequently spoke about being adopted when we were younger. I told her we only talked about it one time as kids and then had not spoke about it again until six months ago. She made a comment about us avoiding the subject because of the pain. I started to get angry. I told her I *did not* have pain in my life until the day she called me 15 years earlier. The truth: I was not *aware* of the pain. I now know it was there; I just didn't know it then.

We also talked about my mother offering to show Diane our family photos. I was not ready to do it but maybe my mother was. I said that perhaps I was standing in the way of the two of them saying things to each other they needed to say.

Diane and I hung up and I went to bed. I woke up in the morning with an image in my head. It was of a wall, a castle wall. It had holes in it, maybe from cannonballs. Stuff, liquid, was pouring out of the holes. I sat at my desk and hand-wrote an essay titled, "The Wall." It flowed out of me almost as one complete sentence. I didn't read it until I was completely finished. (The following is exactly as I wrote it, no edits or corrections.)

I don't remember building it. I think it started on day three. It was such a part of me. I felt it was my job to keep it big and strong. I thought it was a good thing. I didn't know what was on the other side.

When I started to have questions, I think the wall took on a life of its own and became bigger and stronger without me knowing it. The wall knew what was on the other side and it wanted to protect me. If I understood that I didn't have to have the wall, that other people didn't have walls, perhaps I wouldn't want it either and I would work to take it down.

In the years when I did have questions, maybe 13 or 14, the wall did its job. I could talk about it with friends and no feelings from the other side of the wall escaped. I can remember feeling curious, wondering why and even once feeling bad. But I can picture the wall during those times and it was in emergency mode, alarms going off, crews working overtime, a loudspeaker saying, "Must fill cracks, need more bricks!" It worked because after that year I didn't express much curiosity again.

There would be the occasional movie, TV show, news story that, when seen, would shoot at the wall, but 18-20 years of hard work made it almost perfect.

Then on August 20, 1992, the wall was blown open by a sneak attack. There were holes everywhere and stuff was oozing out of the holes. I felt sick. I didn't even know until that moment that the wall existed. In a couple months, the wall was repaired and became invisible to me again. Two problems. First, something broken, and then repaired, is often not as good as the original. Second, I was not able to put everything back behind the wall before it was repaired. Some stuff stayed out and caused confusion, hurt and sadness. Because it was only a little bit of the stuff, I didn't even know why it was there in the first place. I couldn't put it back behind the wall so it would need a new hiding place. I didn't have one so I created one by getting bigger myself.

Over the years, other people tried to remove a few bricks but I was afraid, remembering what was behind the wall hurt.

Only when God worked on the wall did I listen, and probably not as many times as He asked. And probably with not the effort that He was looking for.

In 1999, I tried to have contact without moving the wall. It seemed okay to share a few things, gain some knowledge. But the whole time I was protecting the wall, it had become a friend, I didn't want to lose it. When questions came and she tried to tell me about the stuff on the other side of the wall, it hurt too much and this time I helped the wall. I put up reinforcements; I made sure we would be okay.

In March of 2007, the letter came and all of a sudden, the wall cracked. I can see now that God was trying to bring the wall down. But first, I had to see the wall. It was such a part of me I couldn't tell where I left off and it began. God had put people in my path who would help me. When the people helped, I could finally see the wall. It was larger than life. Thirty-eight years of building had proven very successful.

In time, the wall cracked, bricks fell, and sometimes huge sections fell all at once. The stuff came pouring out from behind the wall but because I never knew what was behind the wall I didn't recognize any of it. It would take months for me to understand things that had been inside me my whole life. It hurt; sometimes the sections that fell came right down on my heart causing so much pain.

*I could now see, how over the years, working to rebuild the wall, had not really helped me and I knew it was time to try to live without the wall. In my mind, I actually remember seeing it for the first time. It was never ending. I thought it protected me. And I suppose during the years that I didn't know it existed, it did protect me. Once I saw it, the enormity of it, I realized it only held me back. During those months, the wall **fell** sometimes, but other times I actively worked to take it apart. So in my mind what is left is not a wall. It is a structure with windows. I think it is a small structure and I can see what is inside. Hurt and pain and anger still live there but I see them and I recognize who they are. They have lived there for so long I am afraid to have them leave me completely. Who will I be without them in my life? I think I know. I caught glimpses of this person over the summer. She is happy and free. Others saw these things in me and told me how great I looked. Even after the wake, someone said that I, of course, looked sad, but at the same time, looked whole and healthy and beautiful. So, that is who I am, or at the very least who I **can** be if I can let it happen.*

I shared my essay with my sister, Carolyn and Mary. They were all supportive of my feelings.

*   *   *

I am not sure what the clinical definition of a nervous breakdown is, but over the course of the next week, I probably came close. We were all struggling with the recent events and little things pushed me over the edge. Katie had a tantrum at the dentist's office. Allison gave me attitude when I questioned her about her homework. Dirty dishes were everywhere. There was nothing to cook for dinner and the kids kept telling me they were hungry. Then, in walked the straw that broke the camel's back. Murph came in the house holding his motorcycle helmet. I knew this meant he wanted to go drop off his bike at the dealership for a modification. I knew this meant he would need me to follow him and give him a ride home. A spilled drink sealed the deal. I lost it.

"Why is it that I am the only person who can pick anything up around here? I am so sick of having to do everything! Would it kill you guys to clean up after yourselves?" I had a complete tantrum in my kitchen, nobody was safe, I yelled at everyone. The kids went to their rooms in tears. "How could you possibly walk in here with your helmet? Did you even ask if we had time to do that tonight? Where are your priorities? Find somebody else to pick you up because I am not going! I am too busy cooking and cleaning!"

By this time, I was in tears and ready to collapse. I felt terrible. Once I calmed down, I brought the kids back out and we all sat at the table. I apologized over and over. I told the kids I was feeling overwhelmed and out of control. I said it was far easier to yell and scream about homework and unfinished chores when I really wanted to yell my heart was broken. My brother died and there was nothing I could do to change it. I apologized repeatedly. I told them I needed help to deal with those feelings and I was talking to Jenny and seeing a grief counselor at Hospice.

I had an appointment with Jenny the next day. I was anxious to tell her about the long conversation with Diane and about writing "the wall." I told Jenny that, years earlier I worked with a little girl who had significant problems with defiance. One day the mother said to me, "I feel like she is a colt and needs to be broken." Driving to Jenny's office that day those words went through my head. *I* felt broken. The part of me that had been fighting this for so long was ready to be done. The part of me that has been okay with everything was ready to be in charge. I would try to listen more to my heart.

*   *   *

I found myself again in one of those spaces where I talked to anyone who would listen. In a conversation with my father-in-law, I told him I had made my peace with his wife before she died. I had made my peace with Danny before he died. I want to learn my lesson!!! I don't want to have to go back and make peace anymore. I want to live my life in a way that allows me to be open. On my way home, I felt compelled to share all of this with Ray, Richard and Diane. Not on the phone, it would need to be in person. I called Diane the next day and asked if she would meet me on Sunday in Schroon Lake. She agreed without asking me why I needed to see her.

We met in the village and went down by the beach to talk. There were no picnic tables so we sat side by side on a bench. I told her how I woke up the morning after our phone call with the image of the wall. I pulled out my essay and read it to her. It was emotional and I cried a few times. She put her hand on my back. I finished and told her about feeling broken, like the colt, about not wanting to have to go back and make peace, just wanting to live my life without anger. I did not want to feel like I had to be so guarded.

Diane thanked me for all I had said. She told me she loved me and she always felt connected to my parents. They were all grateful for the same thing—me. She said she found it settling that both she and my mother were able to have what they had hoped for as young women. Diane had been able to have more children, keep them and raise a family. My mother had been able to conceive and carry her own baby. We embraced and she took my face into her hands. She told me again how much she loved me and how beautiful I was. It was the longest eye contact I ever allowed. It was cold out and we were both shivering. I suggested we go to a diner. We ordered and then ate.

After the plates were cleared, I told Diane that I wanted to share something with her. I truly had made progress. I felt confident and steady as I took my baby book from the bag. I could see the emotion on her face. I can imagine that she was excited and scared at the same time. She remained calm, although seeing the pictures of when I was little was obviously difficult. As she turned the page, she saw a photo of me when I was 6 or 7 months old; she reached over and held my wrist. This was one of the few times that I was able to stare and study her reactions. I was not afraid of what she was thinking. I guess I thought that she would be so engrossed I could be that proverbial fly on the wall. She asked a few questions along the way, not many. My baby book only contains about 20 photos. There is a great deal more documentation about my life. My mother wrote pages about me using the first person as if I wrote them myself. Diane did not appear to read too much of it. She finished looking at it and I put it away. I excused myself to the ladies room to wash up and when I returned, she did the same.

As she came back to the table she said, "If you ever want to call me something else besides Diane it would be okay. And in time, if the kids want to call me something else, if they want another grandmother that would be okay." I froze! My body seized into one big muscle. I could not even look at her.

I replied, "That is a lot to think about for today." I felt like I pushed a pause button on the rest of the world so I had time to think. I could picture myself with Jenny telling her what had just happened. She would want to know how I responded. In my vision, when Jenny asked what I said to Diane, I told her, "Nothing." I could picture Jenny giving me a look that implied I had missed a valuable opportunity. I pushed the play button on the rest of the world. "I want the memory of today to be a good one, so I am going to say this and then let it go. My biggest fear has been you will want too much from me. I just poured my heart and soul out to you and now you asked for more."

She quickly said, "I didn't mean now, just if ever."

"Even the suggestion is too much."

She said she did not mean to upset me. I told her I knew she didn't mean to, she didn't realize how it would sound to me. It continued to speak to how we are in different places. I was quiet for a few minutes but she continued to talk about something else. I began to feel my body untangle and relax. I commented it was getting late and we should be on our way. We walked out, embraced quickly and headed to our cars parked on opposite ends of the street.

I got in my car and promptly broke into . . . laughter. Had that really just happened? I suppose it spoke to the progress I had made. Months earlier the comments she made would have caused me to run screaming from the diner like my hair was on fire. Once home, I shared the story with my circle of people. Everyone seemed to have the same reaction, glad I had decided to tell Diane of my feelings and intrigued as to why she would choose that moment to share hers.

Over the next two days, I spoke with Ray and Richard. I also wanted to convey to them how I was feeling. I wanted them to know they were important in my life. I think they both felt it was more important that I admitted everything to Diane. More than anyone else, these two men knew what our meeting meant to their mother.

Diane and I exchanged emails for the next week or so, mostly about her comment to me in the diner. She said the comment had not come out as she intended. I inquired as to what it was she wanted to convey. She wrote back, referring to a letter I had sent in 1999 where I had written I was having difficulty referring to her by name and I was uncomfortable with the term biological mother. Her present comment was about letting me know it was okay to call her something else. I wrote back asking what she thought the "something else" should be. I encouraged her to be honest with me. We eventually spoke on the phone on Friday, five days after our meeting. Diane said the comment didn't have as much to do with *calling* her something but *referring* to her, should I be in the position to introduce her. She stated she would feel comfortable introducing me as her daughter. I expressed hesitation. Diane and I continued our phone conversation but much of it was "yeah . . . but" type comments each trying to get the other to see her point. It was obvious the subject was not going to be resolved during this phone call. Diane started to talk about the foster care situation. She had only recently learned about my foster care stay. She thought I left the hospital and went directly to live with my parents. When she learned that was not the case, she was angry; beyond angry, enraged and furious would be better descriptors. It bothered me when she wanted to talk about it. She wanted to talk about how she had not been told, how hard the whole thing had been, how when she signed the papers in the middle of March she thought I was already living with my parents. I asked Diane not to talk about it with me.

*   *   *

Each time I questioned my parents about scattering Danny's ashes they were vague. I eventually called his girlfriend, Karen, to ask when we were doing it. She said the coming weekend was no good because she had to work; the weekend after was not good because of something else. We were not planning a birthday party here; couldn't she clear her schedule for this? I hung up with her and told my parents we should set the date and just tell her it is non-negotiable. They didn't bite. I started to get upset saying if we didn't do it soon, there would be snow. The place Danny wanted to be scattered would be a walk through the woods as it was. I couldn't picture people would want to go in the snow. I was shocked at my parents' reaction. They just said, "Then we'll do it in spring." Not good enough for me; I wanted this over. I wanted closure. I wanted to know there were no more steps to check off on the "What to do when your brother dies" list I had created in my head. My sister and I discussed the matter and neither of us had a very good feeling about it. We didn't know very much about Karen. It didn't seem smart to count on still being in touch with her come spring.

*   *   *

At my next appointment with Jenny, I told her of my visit with Diane and the comments she made at the diner. I told Jenny how hard it was to hear Diane talk about the past, and how difficult it was for her to make her decision and how long she had looked for me etcetera, etcetera, and etcetera. It was especially hard to hear her upset about my placement in foster care. Jenny asked why it was so hard to hear. I said I thought I had heard it enough. She promptly said, "That is what you THINK, how do you FEEL?" My second comment must have only been a paraphrase of the first because Jenny repeated her question. When I couldn't think of a different answer, I suggested we table the discussion.

On the way home, I continued to think about what I felt. It struck me that I felt hurt. Every time Diane spoke of the adoption, signing papers, her anger with the system, it all hurt. I ended up sending the following email to Diane.

I saw Jenny today, the first time since our meeting in Schroon Lake. She was happy to hear all that happened between us. I talked about how we continue to be in different places. In all these 15 years, I feel you have always had a clear picture of what you want our relationship to be. I have never had a sense of what I want it to be. When I started gong to Jenny back in March, my goal was to figure out why I had not faced this situation in all these years. Once I knew I could not face it because of anger and hurt, I had to figure out why I had those feelings. Once I figured out why I had those feelings, because of being surrendered, I had to find a way to get over those feelings. I knew I did not want them in my life. Indeed much has happened in these months; sometimes it is quite unbelievable.

I talked today of having a hard time when you tell me over and over about your decision to place me for adoption and how you gave me up out of love. How you wanted me to have what you could not provide. Jenny asked me how I feel when you say those things. I commented that I had heard it enough, I believed you, I accepted why you made the decision. I could put myself in your shoes and see why you did it. Her answer to that was, "That is what you think, but what do you FEEL." I didn't have an answer. As I drove home, some ideas came to mind.

I have shared with you that I didn't even know I had these feelings until very recently. So even though that wound of being surrendered is very old, I only saw it a few months ago. Each time you tell me about your decision, how you wanted to give me more but couldn't, I feel like it rips open the wound again. It hurts. I need time to let the wound heal, time when we don't discuss the past. I don't know that I can be the sounding board that you seem to need.

What I can say it this, I believe you. I believe you did the best you could with the knowledge you had at the time. I believe you wish you could have made a different decision if it were at all possible. I believe you love me. I believe you wanted, and continue to want, the best for my family and me.

I ask this, stop telling me about the past. Maybe there will be times when it is relevant to the conversation and then it will be okay. It seems sometimes you want to tell me over and over so I will see how much you care. I think about the day at Jenny's when you showed me all the papers and receipts. I think you show me things and tell me about your search for me and all that went into it, so I will see how much you love me. You think it will help me accept you. In reality, it is too much.

I don't know if it is the same, but perhaps a comparison would be the situation almost 15 years ago. I wrote a letter telling you that I did not want to be in contact. I know that my decision at that time hurt you. I was not trying to hurt you but I know my action was not what you wanted.

So, I guess picture if I talked about how I made that decision and why I made that decision as frequently as your telling me about your decision from 38 years ago. I can imagine each time I talk about that time, you can recall getting my letter and how you felt on that day.

I can't say I have a memory of 38 years ago, but I guess I have an appreciation of what it might have felt like. When you start talking about being in the hospital, signing the papers or your search for me, what I hear in my heart is, "Remember that time when I left you." I don't think I always feel that way and I am certain there will be times in the future when it won't feel that way, but for now it does.

Diane, I believe you. You love me. I need more time and more space to see where the road takes me. So the time and space is not time away from you, but time away from the wound. Give it time to heal. My heart is a little battered and beaten after these recent weeks. As the saying goes though, "God will heal your broken heart if you give him all the pieces." Perhaps that is what we both need to understand, YOU do not need to heal me, and I do not have to heal you. God will let us know what to do.

Christine

I did not hear anything back right away. A couple days later, I received a call from Ray. He said that Richard was headed to Diane's house for a weekend visit. He would soon be leaving for a five-week medical rotation in Alaska. Ray wondered if we could all get together. After many phone calls, it was decided we would meet at Diane's house. Murph and the kids agreed to go with me. In the end, Ray was not able to attend because of his daughter's hockey practice.

Before leaving our house, I took a picture from a frame in Allison's room. It was a photo of me given to my parents when they adopted me. We do not know who took it, but I am probably 6 to 8 weeks old. Diane once told me on the Mother's Day after I was born, she received a photo of me in the mail. It sounded to be similar to the photo my parents were given. Over 30 years earlier, when Diane's husband left, he took a small wooden box from her nightstand. Her only photo of me was in that box.

While we visited, the kids took turns using Diane's automatic juicer creating some very interesting concoctions. Various combinations of celery, carrot, apple, melon and mango juices were brought out in shot glasses for tasting. They were clearly having fun and I did take some satisfaction in knowing the visit was a positive interaction for them.

Diane began to talk a little more about her plans for a group cruise. She showed us mementos from her previous voyage. I was a little nervous about the conversation, as we had not yet committed to going. When she asked about the kids' school vacation dates, I looked them up on her computer. She was overjoyed when our February vacation was the same as her granddaughter's break. I could feel my hesitancy growing.

Before we left, I was alone in the kitchen with Diane. I pulled the photo out of my pocket. I told her that I remembered the story about my photo and the wooden box. She took a brief glance at it and I could tell she was too emotional to study it. She walked out of the room and we did not talk about it again. Jenny later asked me why I gave it to Diane. Why not ask for a copy to be made? I told her the photo was not very important to me. It obviously meant far more to Diane, she should have it.

*   *   *

Each time I spoke with Ray or Diane they mentioned the cruise. I was so tentative. I was still having trouble being comfortable in the same room with Diane for any length of time. Could I possibly handle going on vacation with her and 10 other members of her family? My friends teased me a little about the vacation being a cruise, saying Diane was going to get me out into the middle of the ocean where I would not be able to escape. On the serious side, many also pointed out that cruise ships are huge. They assured me that there would be more than enough space to have privacy.

Danny's death eventually persuaded me to go on the trip. It had convinced me that life could turn on a dime sometimes. After my lumpectomy, I had vowed not to take things for granted. I had taken Danny's life for granted. I assumed he would be around forever. Now he was gone and I would give anything to have one more day with him. My anxiety about going on the cruise was outweighed only by my fear of *not* going. I worried, if I did not go, someday I would regret it. When I finally did decide that we were interested, I couldn't come right out and say it. I was on the phone with Ray and I said everything except, "We will go." Instead, I said things like, "We are thinking we might do it. It seems like we might want to go. We are thinking it sounds possible." Luckily, Ray could decipher my non-committal statements and told Diane that we were in. She called a few days later stating that she had it narrowed down to two cruises and wanted our input. We were actually going to go; we were going on a cruise with my birth family during the February break.

*   *   *

In addition to seeing Jenny, I was also going to grief counseling at our local Hospice. I figured Jenny had enough to handle just dealing with the Diane situation. I met Maureen when we went to counseling with the kids after Murph's mom died. I am sure I was not the first person to tell her an after-years-of-a-difficult-relationship-we-made-our-peace-six-months-ago type story. When I first went, I told Maureen I had come to terms with Danny's death. It was his time. He is better off in heaven. Now he can be at rest. Doesn't all of that sound incredibly healthy? My expectations for Maureen were similar to those I had when I first went to see Jenny. I wanted her to say, "Wow, what a story. Yes, I think you are fine. Two and a half weeks is the perfect amount of time to mourn someone. You have my permission to be done with it. Thanks for stopping by." (Go ahead and laugh. I know you want to.) I told Maureen it was not Danny's death, but his *life* that I was trying to reconcile. I told her about Jenny and the situation with Diane. Like most people I met, her comment was, "You have a lot going on, don't you?" I shared with her all I was thinking on the night Danny died, the things I didn't have the chance to tell him. She had me write a letter to him. I cried as I wrote. I wrote that I wanted to help him. I was sorry that I stayed away from him for so long. I was sorry that I did not always accept him for who he was. I thanked him for his gift of forgiveness.

*   *   *

In November, I planned to attend a speech conference in Boston. Some time away from my family responsibilities and a chance to connect with friends would probably do me some good. A few nights before I left, my mother called. She was talking really fast. "I guess you should know, blah, blah, blah, and since she knows you should hear it from me, blah, blah, blah Karen is pregnant." I was speechless. Good thing my mother was not, she continued to speak even though I had said nothing. "She found out a couple weeks ago; she said they were trying to have a baby." This statement was almost more shocking than the first one. Trying to have a baby? She and Danny were both over 40. They each had three children from previous relationships. Neither was too good about holding down a job. Danny was having trouble with alcohol again. To me, this did not sound like a stable situation for a new life. My mother hung up. As I stood there, dumbfounded, I felt sick. I felt as if Danny reached right through the grave, took hold of me and shook me conveying, "You don't get rid of me that easy."

I called Martha. She knew it was me before she answered. Her voice was flat, no emotion. "Can you believe it?" was her greeting to me. We spoke for only a minute. I started to get angry, more like enraged. I told Murph and then called Stacie and Carolyn. I opened with, "Hollywood can't write this kind of stuff!" Secretly, I wondered if it was even true. I did not sleep well that night.

The next morning I called my mother to see how she was. I spoke of my upset saying how could they possibly *decide* to have a baby with all their other problems. She started to talk about it being God's plan. I yelled at her, "There is no way God would allow this to happen!" Perhaps I needed to work, just a bit more, on being less judgmental. Throughout the day, I continued to obsess about the situation. It was a progression of thoughts getting more negative each time. Danny was not a good father to the children he already had. Danny was an absentee father to the children he already had. Danny did not take care of the children he already had. Danny *abandoned* the children he already had. With that thought, I heard a, "BINGO" somewhere in the atmosphere. When my anger pushed me toward the word abandoned, I knew I was in fact upset about my own abandonment. I had trouble with this all my life. I cannot stand to leave something behind. I once went to every house in the neighborhood trying to figure out who owned a stray cat. The news of a baby had enraged me because Danny's death was the ultimate abandonment. No future reunion for this baby. No future reunion for me. Of course, I believe in heaven, I believe Danny is there and I believe I will see him again someday. However, right then I did not want to be rational, I just wanted to be mad.

*   *   *

I had a session with Maureen a few days after the Boston conference. I told her that I had not cried for weeks after Danny's death and then, the other day the floodgates opened and I could not stop. I was driving and heard a song about heaven. Suddenly an image of Danny appeared in my head. He was dancing around, very happy. I began to cry uncontrollably. The hurt I experienced was almost as bad as the night he died. Maureen asked, "When you feel upset, where do you feel it physically?" I had to think for a second and then told her it was pain in my chest. She told me that in watching me, she noticed that I frequently hold my breath. After she brought it to my attention, I noticed she was right. After that, I tried to remind myself to breathe. As if I didn't have enough to do already.

Late November brought about two difficult days, Thanksgiving and Danny's birthday. On Thanksgiving, my parents traditionally made the rounds, breakfast at my house and then dinner at Danny's. We usually had a whole family celebration about a week later to celebrate Danny and Martha's birthdays, which were only ten days apart. This year, we had a slightly varied turkey-day. I hosted a breakfast at our house and then Martha had a dinner later in the day. We went over for dessert. The day went fairly well, except for when my mom started announcing to everyone that Karen was pregnant. My friends and neighbors just looked at me wide-eyed. I just shook my head as if to say, "Don't ask, we'll talk about it later."

Earlier in the day, I spoke with my Aunt Marge. I told her about our decision to go on the cruise. She thought it was great and she ended our call with this; "Crissy you have more than enough love inside you to go around. I think it is wonderful." Each time I heard a comment like that, it was like a chisel chipping away another piece of the cement that had been protecting my heart.

The night after Thanksgiving, Murph and I went to Mary's house for poker. It was quite the evening and I proceeded to have too much to drink. As the hours passed, I eventually started to talk with the other guests about Diane and Danny. I talked about Diane's call to me 15 years earlier, my decision to meet her in June and my plans to have her meet my family at the end of September. Much of the conversation is a fuzzy memory, but I do vividly remember saying, "I was all set to have them meet and then do you know what my brother did? HE UP AND DIED!" Perhaps I was not dealing with his death as well as I thought.

Right after Thanksgiving, my parents' neighbor, my "Aunt" Barb, went into the hospital. She was diagnosed with lung cancer, stage 4. I had already lived that nightmare with my mother-in-law. I was devastated to think of these people, people I cared a great deal about, having to go through the same terrible ordeal. I visited with her in the hospital three or four times. I tried to assist Annette, her daughter, with questions for the doctors and suggestions to help her dad.

In the midst of all this, my mother told us that Karen was going for an ultrasound. The appointment was on the 27th, Danny's birthday. If I were in her position, I think I would have declined that appointment and asked for a different day, but who am I to judge? Late in the day on the 27th, I called my mother to ask about the ultrasound. She said that Karen told her it had been postponed. None of this sat well with Martha or me, we were getting suspicious. The following Monday, Martha called me early in the morning. She had just received a call from Mom. Karen had a miscarriage. I didn't know what to think, but I knew how I felt, relieved.

                    *   *   *

In mid-December, Richard was set to graduate as a physician's assistant. He invited me to the ceremony. It was about four hours from my house. I left early in the morning to get there for the 11 a.m. service. I came in with only a moment or two to spare. Diane had actually been watching for me by a different entrance so I had to introduce myself to Diane's brother and Richard's friends. The service started right away so there wasn't time for small talk. After the diplomas were handed out, there was a reception. Richard had achieved a special honor and we were all invited to take part in a luncheon. During our meal, different professors and administrators approached the table to congratulate Richard. Each time he would go around the table introducing everyone. It was the same each time: this one, that one, this one, that one, my mother Diane . . . (watch out here it comes), "my sister Christine." Each time my reaction was the same, a polite smile, a nod of acknowledgement and a churning in my stomach. After the lunch, we all went to Richard's house. I presented him with a small gift, a framed photo from our day at Moose Pond. He was clearly touched. When it was time to leave, Diane presented me with Christmas gifts for each of the kids as well as a basket and homemade jam for my parents.

As a Christmas gift to Diane, I made a collage with photos of Richard's graduation along with portions of the program noting his special honor. I sent Ray the photo from Moose Pond as well as the photo from the day in Burlington when he met the kids for the first time.

We all continued with our Christmas plans. I have to say we were all faring pretty well. Mom was shopping and baking, Martha and I made last minute plans for our holiday meal. On the first night of their school vacation, the kids were spending the night at my parents' and I went out for dinner with Rana. Halfway through my second beer, my cell phone rang and it was Allison. She was frantic. My parents' neighbor, my "Aunt" Barb, had died. Unbelievable.

Seeing my upset, Rana offered to drive me to my parents' house. I went in to see my mom and she said Dad was across the street with "Uncle" Al. I went over, walked in and gave my dad and Al each a hug. I had been so concerned that this family would have to endure the same long, drawn out battle my in-laws did. Barb's cancer battle was cut short by either a heart attack or a stroke. In my opinion, a tremendous blessing, but I am sure her family could not see it that way, especially not in those initial hours. I was impressed watching my dad interact with Al. Dad had made the initial call to the funeral home, was looking up doctor's numbers and was providing so much emotional support. During the first hours after my brother's death, Dad had been so distant and disconnected. I had to imagine, that like me, he was feeling a flashback of sorts. I was impressed by his ability to put all of that aside and help our friends. I waited for Annette to arrive and sat with them for a while. We talked about what they would need for the funeral home and what decisions they would have to make immediately and which ones could wait a day or two. Annette asked me to help her write the obituary. I told her I would stay the night at my mom's and she should call if she needed me. My mom was still awake and we sat and visited for a while. Mom had known Barb for over 40 years. This was less than three months from losing Danny. I was worried about her. Annette called and was not feeling well. I eventually took her to the emergency room as we felt she needed an IV and perhaps something to calm her nerves. Standing there in the ER, I had flashbacks to seeing Danny. I saw the nurse who had been the one to tell us about Danny's death, too much reality. I was relieved when Annette's husband arrived. I went home after 4 a.m. having not yet gone to bed. I slept a couple hours and then got up and went to work.

The wake for Barb was two days before Christmas, and the funeral was Christmas Eve. As we sat in the funeral home before the church service, one of my parents' neighbors commented that her daughter would be meeting us at the church. In my mind I thought, Danny should be along any minute too. It was a reality check that hit me like a slap in the face. I started to cry and I bet others figured I was sad about Barb. As my mother got me a tissue I wanted to look at her but couldn't. I am certain she was feeling the same way, expecting Danny to walk through the door and sit down next to us. It was an unbearable déjà vu. We were in the same church where Danny's funeral was held. The priest used the same readings. Afterwards we went to the same restaurant for brunch. Many of the attendees were the same too. I think people were afraid to talk to us. They had to know that even though we were there for Barb, our grief for Danny was still so close to the surface. We did what we could to be of comfort, but quite honestly, our reserves were a little low.

After the brunch, it was time to snap back to reality. It was Christmas Eve. A few more presents to buy and several tins of cookies to deliver. We went to the 7 p.m. mass with my parents. I was allright except when I looked at my mother, which I could not stop doing.

I spoke with Diane late on Christmas Eve. It was a short conversation. I was exhausted and she could hear it. She told me how much she liked the collage I had sent. She wished me well, we hung up and I went to sleep.

On Christmas morning, we opened gifts with the kids first and then my parents came over with my sister and her family. Martha and I planned a trick for our father's gift. He wanted a fish finder. We purchased a general gift card and attached it to a fish Christmas ornament. First, she hid clues at her house for their morning breakfast. The final clue at her house explained that he needed to come to my house. Once at my house we had him looking room to room and finally a clue asked him to find the fish ornament. Taped to the back was our note, "Wouldn't this have been easier with a fish finder?" This whole scavenger hunt scheme was an homage to our childhood Easter basket hunts. My father, or should I say the Easter Bunny, hid our baskets and then left written clues leading us to the secret hiding place. We all had a good laugh about the fish finder and my parents were once again models for positive attitudes. We had much to be grateful for in life. I was indeed grateful for my family and my friends who had provided so much support. For Christmas, Mary gave me a Willow Tree figurine. On the top of the box, she wrote she thought of me immediately when she saw it. It was an angel with her arms outstretched above her head. The name of the statue was "Courage."

New Year's Eve was a significant night. We were again at Mary's for a party and I talked about being ready to "close the book" on 2007. We were standing on the back porch when one of Mary's friends arrived. When Julie saw me, she pointed and smiled saying, "Lifetime movie." I had to imagine that was my new nickname after my "tell all" at the previous party.

Chapter 7

MOVING FORWARD

We started out 2008 with goals of saving money for the cruise and working out to lose weight, also for the cruise. By the time we left in mid-February, we had saved nearly two hundred dollars in loose change and I had lost seventeen pounds, success on both fronts.

During one workout, I was struggling. I didn't think I could make it to the end of the pre-programmed treadmill course. I stared down at the numbers seeing just how much more torture I had to endure. As I looked back up, I saw my brother standing right in front of me, plain as day. He was wearing jeans and a flannel shirt and he had that usual smile on his face; the expression I called his "shit-eating grin." He looked at me and said, "You can do it." And I did.

After I finished the workout, I felt compelled to draw a picture. Literature I had been reading, suggested writing and drawing with your non-dominant hand to tap into deeper emotions. I had never considered doing it before, but for some reason, I felt now was the time. I grabbed a piece of paper to draw a bird. When my brother was no longer in front of me, I had the image of a bird in my head. First, I went to draw the wings. After I drew them, I realized they were not the correct perspective. I wanted them from the side not the front. I moved down the paper and sketched the side view of a bird with a bag in its mouth. As I looked at what I had drawn, my eyes went back up to the first set of wings. I realized they looked angelic. I added a head and a flowing gown. I wanted to know what it all meant. After a few minutes, I decided the angel was God and the bag in the bird's mouth was all the negative history I had with my brother. God was taking it away from me; I no longer needed to worry about it.

*   *   *

Ray and I were on the phone one night and he asked me to hold as he clicked over to another caller. When he returned, he had a different tone in his voice. I asked if everything was all right. He said the call was from his mother's boyfriend, asking his permission to propose marriage to Diane. Ray was over 36 years old and Diane had been a single mom for almost all his life. I once asked Diane if she dated throughout the years. She told me she hadn't. She said that her emotions about my adoption had left her so unsettled. She didn't think she could open her life to a romantic relationship. Last summer, after our meeting, Diane started dating. The man was someone she had known through her church for over 25 years. He had asked her out several times in recent years, but she always declined. A couple months after their first date, Diane told me that meeting me had finally put some issues to rest, she felt ready for a relationship. Now she was getting married! A few days later, Diane called me about some cruise details; I congratulated her on her engagement. I had not met her fiancé yet and I wondered if he would go on the cruise too. I joked with Ray; he would now have three new stepsiblings. Laughing I said, "Boy you are getting new siblings all over the place."

*   *   *

In January my mother voiced she wanted Danny's ashes back for lent so she could pray over them. I told her I would get in touch with Karen. I called one night; the phone just rang and rang no machine. I called her cell phone and got voice mail. I left a message saying that I needed to talk to her about something important; she called back three minutes later. I was nervous as I asked how she was doing. Enough small talk, I got down to business. "It is going to be lent soon and Mom would really like the ashes so she can pray over them."

"Okay, I will bring them over on Monday."

"Are you sure? I can drive out tonight and get them. I don't want you to go out of your way."

"No, I'll stop Monday after work."

"Well, thank you very much. I also bought Mom a special keepsake box and I would like his wallet and birth certificate to be in there."

"Sure, I'll bring them too."

We ended our call and I let my mother know to expect everything back in a couple days. I called my mother Tuesday morning and she said that Karen had not come. Mom blew it off saying, "Well the roads were icy last night." My blood pressure jumped a few points. I asked if Karen had called, or just didn't show up. It was the latter. My blood pressure jumped a few more points. I told my mother that I would take care of it. She started yelling at me to leave it alone, that it wasn't that important. Remember how my mother does not like to "make waves?" Our argument lasted a few more minutes and ended with my mother hanging up on me. In the middle of my workday, I drove out to Karen's house. Nobody was home and it looked like no one had been there in some time. Dozens of envelopes were stuffed in the mailbox. I noticed a rotten pumpkin on the porch. It was now over two months since Halloween. I looked through the window of the front door. I could see things still in the house, furniture and pictures on the wall. I wondered if Danny's ashes were in there, maybe only a few feet on the other side of the door. Could I just go in and get them myself? Would that be stealing? My parents were legally the next of kin and they *had* paid for the funeral, the ashes belonged to them, right? I tried the door; it was locked. I didn't know if I should go around to a different door. The whole place felt cold and creepy. I decided to leave.

The next day my mother called. She said that she and my father had decided to drive out to Karen's house to get the ashes. I told her that I had gone the day before and the place looked deserted. She was surprised. I was still upset about our argument from the day before so I didn't offer too much more. By the end of the week, I had heard nothing from Karen and she didn't return my calls, it was disturbing. I tried a little experiment. I called from someone else's house so it wouldn't be my number on the caller ID. I was shocked when Karen answered her phone on the second ring. When she realized it was me, she said she didn't have time to talk, but would call me later. I ended by saying, "I *hope* I hear from you Karen." She never called.

We heard via the grapevine that Karen was being evicted. If she did not pay her back rent, the landlord would take possession of all the contents of the house. We still didn't know if the ashes were there. I felt a complete lack of control with this situation. All of my brother's possessions were in that house. My mother had paid for lots of things in that house. Now we were going to lose them all because Karen was being evicted. I called my sister. I suggested we strike a deal with Karen and the landlord. We would pay whatever she owed for back rent with the agreement we get all of Danny's things and all the items my mother purchased. Martha recommended that we should wait to see how the court proceedings played out. I started crying. I felt responsible because I had been the one to let Karen pick up the ashes. If I hadn't done that, we wouldn't be in this boat. I hung up with her and within minutes, my brother-in-law called. He encouraged me to find peace with Danny's death. He was already gone. Getting the ashes back would not change that. I stated I was trying to take care of Mom too. She wanted some of the stuff back. He said we had all made choices that led us to this point, Danny, my parents and me too.

I spoke with Maureen at Hospice about our situation. I told her how it pained me to think of having to paw through things to find a memento. In our society, when a person dies, his possessions are cherished and carefully distributed to his loved ones. Our scenario was disrespectful and uncivilized. Karen had not been living at the house for some time so she deserted everything, everything it seemed including the ashes. I knew my brother was dead and the box contained just his ashes, but I could not help feel he was all alone in the house, lonely, cold and abandoned.

* * *

The situation with the ashes would have to be on hold for a while as we approached our vacation. My parents came over a few days before the cruise for Katie's birthday. My mother handed me a large manila envelope. Inside were a small wooden boat, a check and a note telling us to have fun on the trip. While I was very appreciative of the financial gift, I was even more thankful for the note as I felt she had given us her blessing to go.

We spent the next days getting everything ready, physically and emotionally. I had a bit of a breakdown right before we left. One morning I told Mary I was afraid to accept Diane, Ray and Richard into my life. I felt if I fully allowed them in, to the level they had hoped for, it would somehow nullify my parents, brother and sister. I had to think back to Murph's comment 15 years earlier, the night of the very first call. My immediate reaction to the call was so intense he could only figure my parents had been killed. Maybe that is what I truly felt in that moment; Diane's contact with me somehow removed my parents from my life. I probably should have gone to more than *two* counseling sessions all those years ago.

I was nervous about spending so much time with everyone in such close quarters. Our rooms on the ship were all right next to each other. A few days earlier, I spoke with Ray, Richard and Diane. I asked if they introduced us to others, or referred to us, that they just use our first names, everyone in our group certainly knew who I was, no reason to point out the obvious. They each said they understood my anxiety and would do the best they could to make me feel comfortable. Ray suggested I not tie myself in knots and focus on having fun. Diane's sister and brother-in-law would also be on the trip. There would be 16 in our group.

I saw Jenny a few days before the trip. She was surprised when we barely spoke about the cruise. I told her I felt ready to go. Before ending the session, I wanted to thank Jenny for all she had done. I told her I could remember 11 short months ago, when I walked into her office. I demanded she stop saying the word "relationship," because I thought I might throw up. Now I was about to go on a vacation with my birth family. I knew I had worked hard to get to this point, but without her direction, I don't think I could have done it. I was so appreciative. She wished me luck.

*   *   *

The day before our trip, Mary asked me to stop by school. She handed me a gift bag and inside was a journal. Inside the front cover, she wrote; "Remember that you are never alone. Write all your thoughts and feelings in this journal while on your trip (I don't want to miss a thing!) Keep God's word in your heart. Some Words I live by: 'Dear Lord, I know that as long as you are there to guide me and express yourself through me I will never be alone in any difficulty.' From Joshua 1:9—'Do not be terrified or discouraged for the Lord, your God will be with you wherever you go.' Also, He is all I need when I need it all." She ended by telling me to have a great trip. Relax, enjoy and be happy! I did in fact fill the pages of that journal with our high seas adventure.

My parents agreed to drive us to the airport in Connecticut, as we could not get a flight out of Albany. We left our house at 1 a.m. to be ready for a 5:30 flight. Everything went off without a hitch. Our flights were on time. We went from Hartford to Philadelphia and onto Tampa. We had paid for bus transfers from the airport to the cruise ship. With three kids in tow and no knowledge about boarding procedures, I did not want to take any chances. In a span of ten hours, we had been in five states and were soon on the Lido deck enjoying drinks and lunch. We met up with Diane and the group almost immediately. There was so much going on and so many people around that there was no time to be nervous or anxious. We met Diane's sister and her husband. Everyone seemed to be at ease. The kids changed quickly and were in the pool before we were even out of the port. After getting settled in our room, Murph and I changed too, and we all went back up to the pool. It was lovely to be sitting in the sun on a February day.

The ship was big but the kids quickly found their way around. We had dinner, explored the arcade, saw a show and went to bed. I had been up for 22 hours. I took a minute to write in the journal about our events of the day; everything was positive. Before we went on the trip, I arranged for flowers to be in Diane's room with a thank-you note. I went on the website everyday for three weeks before I finally committed to the order. They looked nice and she was clearly touched by the gesture. I hoped she wouldn't read too much into it. Oops, did I just say that? Old habits die hard.

Sunday was a full day at sea and we spent the majority of it by the pool. People from our group came and went throughout the day. Diane sat and visited a while, talking about how nice the ship was and such. Each day we had a little newspaper telling us of the day's events. When I saw a "hairy chest" contest, I was sure Murph would win. (Think red-haired ape). He entered thinking it would be fun. One problem, it was not so much a hairy-chest-contest as it was a dance-around-and-make-a-fool-of-yourself contest. For his dignity, I prayed Murph would be one of the first eliminated. He was an excellent sport and his consolation prize, a cruise ship medallion, is a cherished memento. The cruise ship does not tell you (it is probably in the fine print) they videotape everything. For the rest of the voyage, we could watch Murph's performance on closed circuit television; the event was part of a continuous loop reel. That night our whole group ate in the dining room for the formal night. It was exciting to get dressed up. We really did have a good time and I kept thinking there was too much going on to be nervous about anything. It became my mantra.

The next day, Murph, the kids and I went on an excursion to swim with the stingrays and then have lunch on a private beach. It was a remarkable experience. Cole, in particular, enjoyed each minute in the water. He fed the stingrays and then kissed one, which is supposed to be good luck. The water was a lovely shade of blue and the sand was soft beneath our feet. Who could ask for more? We ate at the beach and swam in the warm water. We joked about it being the middle of February. It was probably snowing at home.

Once back on the ship, the girls and I went to the pool. Not long after, I did not feel well. By evening Murph had convinced me to go to the infirmary. A nurse with an English accent started asking many questions; I felt like I was in the care of Mary Poppins. When all was said and done, she gave me a shot to help me stop throwing up. She also sent me back to the room with some pills to take. Getting sick was a lesson in letting go. Before the cruise Ray and Diane had each offered to watch the kids, at any time, should Murph and I want to have a meal alone or go to a show without the kids. While I politely thanked them for the offers, I couldn't picture that I would actually take advantage of it. Let someone else be in control of my kids? I don't think so. I was sick and Murph needed to take me to the doctor. It was dinnertime so the kids went with the rest of the group. I would have to let go of my control.

I was feeling better the next day but still wanted to take it easy. We got off the boat in Mexico and stayed at a little flea market just off the gangway.

The girls got their hair braided and we all bought souvenirs. It was very hot so we quickly got back on the ship and spent the rest of the afternoon by the pool. I told the kids, "Go ahead and tell everyone you went to Mexico, nobody needs to know we were only eight feet inside the border."

We all ate dinner together that night. Diane had hoped there would be one activity each day where we could all be together. Other plans to meet for ice cream or mini golf did not really pan out, but we did eat together more than I had anticipated. The dining room was a great place. Never have I experienced such service. It really is one of those times where, "your wish is my command." This was put into action on the formal night when Katie finished her lobster tail and said, "Mom, I wish I could have another one." Within one minute, a second serving was placed in front of her. Her eyes were big as quarters, a lovely memory.

*   *   *

On our last full day, it rained in the morning. It was actually a nice change as the decks were quiet. We sat under a protected area for breakfast. Murph and Richard visited for a while and I realized how at ease it all felt. We poked around the ship for the rest of the morning trying to visit places we had not seen. The cruise was almost over and I realized I had not spent any time with Diane, just the two of us. I suggested we have lunch together. She seemed happy I asked. During our meal, she asked how we had liked the experience and what the highlights were. As the conversation shifted, she began to talk about her wedding plans. She stated she hoped we would attend. I experienced some slight anxiety, as I wanted to retreat to my old feelings. Thoughts were running through my head: "just because we are on this cruise," "just because I asked you to have lunch," "don't read too much into it." I was able to stop myself though and thought, just experience the moment, don't rush ahead.

Before we went to dinner that night, we had drinks in Richard and Diane's room to celebrate the evening. During dinner, Richard made a toast to Diane for being our hostess as well as wishing her happiness for her upcoming wedding. Everyone was joking around at dinner and there was a lot of laughter. As the waiters sang us a good-bye song, I had to choke back some tears. The cruise had been more than I ever thought it could be (Father Marty had used those *same* words back in September. "Just keep going, and whatever it is that you are working on, it will be more than you think it can be.") The waiter came over with signed placemats for everyone. He had been wonderful at each meal, particularly with the kids. Interestingly enough, his name was Daniel like my brother.

Since it was the last night on the ship, we went all out . . . karaoke! It was an odd feeling (but not so odd) to be joking with Richard about what songs to sing. He shot down each of my suggestions. We eventually settled on "The Gambler" by Kenny Rogers. Richard, Murph and I provided a rendition that will not soon be forgotten. Murph and I then sang "I Got You Babe" but we got confused and I sang the Sonny parts and he sang the Cher parts. Yeah, I know, don't quit our day jobs! During another performance, Richard was dancing with Diane. He came over to me and asked me to dance. It was a bizarre moment. Before we left on the cruise, for some reason, I envisioned Richard asking me to dance. It made me think; I was not sure I had ever danced with Danny. At the time of my own wedding, we were not on good terms. At Martha's wedding things were better between us, but I don't think we danced there either. I turned Richard down saying, "Maybe later." The opportunity did not come up again.

On the way back, I passed Ray's room. His daughter came running out and cheered, "There is a party in Gramma's room." Allison was the next person out of the room and repeated, "There is a party in Gramma's room." I just shot her a look and said, "No." I am sure she was just repeating what the other girl had said but I just could not hear it from her. Quite honestly, this was the only tough moment of the trip. Everything else had gone so well. There was indeed a party in Diane's room. We snacked and had a few more drinks laughing about all the funny moments.

The next morning, everyone was going different directions. I helped Diane bring her suitcases to her sister and brother-in-law's room. They were driving Diane and Richard to the airport. While in the room, Ray stepped out on the balcony and I joined him. He asked how I thought things went. I said we had a great time. Everything had gone better than I could have imagined. I told Ray I wanted a picture with the four of us. I had been afraid Diane would want a lot of pictures with all of us but in fact, my suggestion resulted in the only picture of Ray, Richard, Diane and me. Diane's sister took the photo then we all hugged goodbye. I thanked Diane for the wonderful trip.

*   *   *

I went back to our room to finish packing. We left the boat and went to the airport. Ray, his wife and daughter would be on our flight from Tampa to Philadelphia. When we got to the gate, he was not there, despite leaving quite a bit ahead of us. I called his cell and he told me they were all with Richard and Diane in a café on the other side of security. I was disappointed, that is right, disappointed (who knew?) when I heard we missed the opportunity to spend a little while longer with them. I did not want to put the kids through the process of security again so we stayed put.

I wrote in the journal and made some calls. I spoke with my mom, my aunt, my sister and Mary. They were all thrilled to hear we had fun. Soon enough we were on the plane and headed for the cold northeast. Before we knew it, we were in Albany. Our friend Gary picked us up and the ride home was all a buzz with our adventure. The kids talked about how much fun they had and what they liked best about the cruise. As much fun as it was to be away, I like my house and my things. I was glad to be home. We unpacked what we could and connected the camera to the television so we could see all our photos. We were all excited to see everything again. Ray called to say their flight from Philadelphia to Burlington had been delayed. Then when they finally did get in, their bags were lost. Unfortunately, Ray had put his car keys in his luggage. They had to rent a car to get home. I did not dare tell him our travel had been without incident.

We woke up in the morning to . . . SNOW! Ugh! I called Diane to see when they had made it back from Burlington. I could feel myself holding back a little. She began to talk about all the special memories and so forth and all I could think was, don't gush, please don't gush. I don't think I can handle gushing. Old habits do indeed die a hard death, especially in my home environment.

When Ray saw me on the phone in the Tampa Airport he quipped, "Tell Jenny I said 'hi'," thinking I was already in contact with her. Little did he know I previously scheduled an appointment for the day after we got back. I did go see Jenny on Friday. I showed her all the pictures and the jewelry I bought in Mexico. I told her everything on the trip went really well. I was, however, unsure how to integrate those feelings with everyday life. Sure, it was easy to feel comfortable when you are in the Caribbean, having your every need met. Now I was home, and there was cooking, dishes, laundry and work, could I keep the momentum going? Jenny told me it had been important that I communicated ahead of time with Diane, Ray and Richard. They respected my feelings and that was truly great. She commented in the future, if I ever feel uncomfortable with a situation, I should feel more confident in telling them because they responded this time and likely would again.

We had dinner at my parents' house on Saturday. Murph's dad was there too. We showed them the pictures, hooking the camera up to the big screen television. The kids were practically jumping out of their skin to tell all of the adventures. When our slide show was finished, they all commented it looked like a great time. My mom asked if Diane was happy with the trip. I told her I thought she was, everyone had a lot of fun and Diane seemed glad to share in some of the activities with us.

*   *   *

Over the weekend while watching television, the music video came on for one of my favorite songs, Brad Paisley's "If I Could Write A Letter To Me." In the song, he writes a letter as an adult to himself at 17. Prompted by the song, I decided to write a letter to myself. It would not be to me at 17; it would be to that one-day-old baby inside me. In the journal, I wrote:

> *If I could write a letter to me . . .*
>
> *You will hear you are special, you were chosen, and it was all meant to be. Believe it! Believe all of it! But try not to make it feel like you have to be perfect, that you have to be everything to everyone.*
>
> *Listen to that voice, listen to that whisper, listen to those words you have heard from the beginning of time. You are loved! You are wanted!*
>
> *Protection, don't let it become the most important word in your vocabulary. Let TRUST rise to the top of the list. God will provide for you all you need. When you feel the need to build a wall around yourself, don't do it, because there will be good things that won't find their way in. And when some of those things are gone, they are really gone!*
>
> *Danny, don't hate him, don't ever hate him. He discovered his pain at an early age and perhaps didn't have the courage to face it, the courage you will someday find. The courage you need to make your life whole, the courage you need to heal old wounds.*
>
> *Learn about forgiveness, how to give it as well as how to ask for it. It will provide you with beautiful peace! Nobody is perfect, nobody knows it all, and everyone is doing the best they can.*
>
> *Let go of judgment. Ultimately, you'll only hold yourself back from being the best person you can be.*
>
> *Trust in God's plan. He will put the right people in you path at the right times. When you meet the man of your dreams, (July 29, 1989), let him into your life, all the way. Don't hold back, it is okay to let him take care of you sometimes. Trust in him with your whole heart, he won't let you down. You'll know he and you are meant to be together on several distinct occasions, the three most important being 3/95, 8/96 and 2/00. One look at each of those kids and you'll know it is all as it is supposed to be!*
>
> *Give yourself a break. All of the ups and downs, successes and failures, challenges and mistakes, they all have their place. They all make you who you are, a really good person. Embrace them all as life lessons, learn and grow each day. Learn the difference between wishing something had gone differently and regret. The second is a very strong word, not to be used lightly.*

*In November 2007, you will be offered the opportunity to take a cruise
with your birthmother and your brothers, take it. In February 2008, you
will spend five days with these people and it will change you life, enhance
your life. Trust in the timing and know God has created this path.*

*   *   *

One step forward, two steps back. After all the success of going on the
cruise, I was still feeling anxious about everything. I finally admitted to Jenny
in a phone call that I couldn't cope and perhaps it was time to consider
medication. I researched a few things on the Internet and then went to
my primary doctor. He spoke with me for over an hour. I shared all that
had happened in the recent months. He explained about anti-depressant
and anti-anxiety medications. He gave me some samples and asked me to
come back in a month to evaluate how I was feeling.

I had an appointment with Jenny the next day. I told her how out of
control I felt. I told her how thoughts of Danny and events from his teen
years were bothering me and invading every area of my life.

"Do you think you obsessed on those certain memories?"

"No, I don't think so."

Several hours later, when I was driving my car to work, I recognized
that familiar feeling. Jenny was right on target. I *had* obsessed about things,
events long in the past that should have been buried with Danny. That
was my problem though; we had not buried Danny. We were not even in
possession of his ashes. Earlier, in the session, Jenny encouraged me to find
a creative way to put all those feelings to rest. I remembered how Maureen
at Hospice, had me write letters to Danny. I spent four days writing a
24-page letter to Danny. I told him that I wanted to put things to rest, but
to put them to rest; first, I had to get them out in the open. I wrote about
how his addiction had stolen things from me. His actions had hurt us as
a family and each of us individually. I named three very specific incidents
that had stuck with me for way too long. These were memories that I really
needed to put behind me and get on with my life. I expressed that I had
held onto the past, but now I could make a better choice. I could finally
let those feelings go.

In my creativity, I created a headstone for Danny. I took a cardboard
box and decorated one side in loving and caring language. On the other
side, I wrote all the negative language of addiction I wanted to let go.

On the eve of my birthday it was raining. I asked Murph to make a fire
in our backyard fireplace. As only a loving husband would do, he didn't
ask questions and built me a fire. I took the letter and the headstone out
back. I wondered, if I chose to share my actions with anyone else, would

they think I was crazy? I read the letter aloud to Danny. My voice was soft at first but by the second or third page, I was emphatic, telling him that I would no longer let his difficulties rule my life. When I finished, I stuffed the letter into the headstone box. I looked at the nice side, the one where I drew a boat with a water-skier. I read his name and the nice words I had written. Then I turned it over and read the harsh words. I burned the box along with a pair of jeans that no longer fit since I was losing weight. I wanted to be rid of the old me. The next day was my birthday and it would be the start of new thoughts, feelings and actions. When the fire was out, I took the ashes and put them in an empty coffee jar. I added the small crucifix and the "forgiveness" stone that I had carried for months. I put the top on the jar and buried it in the woods at the back of our yard. I didn't have Danny's real ashes to bury, so I had to create some. I walked back in from the woods, went in the house and went to bed.

*   *   *

I awoke the next morning, a brand new 39-year-old, hoping the events of the night before would magically transform me. This would be the first birthday since meeting my birthmother. I received a card from Diane. Inside was a pair of Claddagh earrings. I lost my breath for a second when I saw them. Years earlier, I was upset when Murph did not do something for my birthday. I confided to a friend, "I don't want much, a few friends over and maybe a pair of Claddagh earrings." There was no way Diane knew that story. This year Murph did a great job of celebrating me. I had four birthday celebrations. On my actual birthday, a Wednesday, I spoke with my parents early in the day because Allison was not feeling well and I wanted to know if she could stay with them for the day. Once I had talked to and seen my parents, I felt like it was okay to call Diane. I was sure she wanted to talk to me but would question if it were acceptable to initiate a call to me. We spoke only a few minutes and I thanked her for the earrings. She told me she purchased them for me a few years back on a trip to Ireland. She did not send them at the time afraid I would not be ready to accept them. She wished me a happy birthday and we said goodbye. That night at home, the kids had cupcakes for me. Richard called to wish me well on turning 40 (ha-ha). Ray did not call on my birthday; it did not surprise me though. Over all the months of talking, he frequently mentioned my birthday as the sixth not the fifth. I was sure he would call tomorrow, and I didn't want to tell him he missed it. He did call on Thursday, and when he found out he had the wrong day, he was so upset with himself. He was headed to the area for guard duty and he joined us for dinner out. He surprised me by paying for the bill on the sly.

On Friday night, Murph had arranged for the kids to spend the night with my parents so we could meet up with friends. The roads were a little slick so only a few people made it but it was lots of fun nonetheless. On Saturday night, we had dinner at my father-in-law's house and my parents came too. My father-in-law handed me a box and inside was a necklace and a pair of earrings. I recognized them right away as my late mother-in-law's. I was so touched he wanted to give them to me. He gave me a lovely card too; I felt very special.

*   *   *

As I have written before, understanding and knowledge come from a variety of resources. I was just about to discharge one of my clients. We only had two sessions left. I was prompting a new word for him and he whined, "That is so hard for me." I thought what a cop-out. A few days later, after a lengthy phone call with a friend, I heard my half of the conversation replay in my head. Repeatedly I heard the same phrase, "This is so hard for me." The fact that I had been "copping-out," was epiphany number 42 on my journey.

Chapter 8

RESOLUTIONS

Once everything settled back into place from the trip, we still had to deal with getting Danny's ashes back. We kept in touch with the landlord and when the court finalized the eviction, he allowed us to come over to the house. I arrived first. It was a cold morning, misty and damp. I walked up to the door and looked inside. The house was completely empty. Where was all the stuff? More importantly, where were the ashes? In all this time, we were not even sure they were there. Terrible thoughts went through my head. Did Karen take them with her? Did she scatter them without telling us? Did she throw them out in the garbage?

My parents arrived right before Martha and Martin. We all stood around doing the same thing, standing with our hands in our pockets, staring at the ground and kicking the dirt. The landlord finally arrived and told us he had emptied the contents of the house into the garage. He opened the door to the house and handed my parents a box that contained Danny's ashes. Thankfully, he had respected the ashes, and didn't heap them into the garage with everything else. He then opened the garage. The complete contents of the house took up the entire space of the garage, floor to ceiling. We had been hopeful we would recover Danny's baby photos, his cookbooks, his wallet and his birth certificate. My mother wanted my nephew's toys. She had given Danny fire trucks, cars, books and puzzles to keep at his house for my nephew. She wanted them all back.

We did not even know where to look for things. Furniture was stacked on furniture, boxes and bins were piled four and five high. There were bags of papers and garbage bags filled with clothes. This was not how I thought it would be. I had pictured us going through dressers, closets and cupboards. I had imagined as I looked through things I would see a shirt or a hat or something which would remind me of Danny, something of his I would want to have. When I think of other special people in my life, I know *exactly* what I would want to remember them. I would want my father's pocketknife, my mother's scapular, and my father-in-law's Cleveland Indians hat. I had no idea if there was *anything* of Danny's I would want. I was hoping something would jump out at me. We started in the front and worked our way back. I eventually climbed over a stack of mattresses to get to the middle of the garage. Martin joined me, climbing over boxes, and holding onto the rafters to steady himself. We uncovered a box of photos. We didn't find the baby photos but we did take a few from the box. We found a bin of my nephew's toys. My mother wanted Danny's boots. I was only able to find one. We found the cookbooks but they were covered in mold, we took them anyway. In the end, we did not find what we wanted but we did have the ashes so the rest didn't really matter. I only took one photo home with me, no shirt and no hat.

The landlord planned to sell everything else at a garage sale. We asked him to keep a lookout for the baby photos and the wallet. We all went home. It was a strange feeling. I suppose it was sadness, that my brother's life had come down to us pawing through bins and boxes, hoping to find a memento. The whole procedure lacked respect. Martin had been right though, Danny made choices in life, and we too made choices that led us to that moment. Each step of this was a new grieving process. We would never have the classic movie scene where the cohesive family all sits together and mourns. It was too painful and I was sure we would probably never speak of this day again.

My mother thought of a few more things she wanted after we left; she returned to the house during the yard sale. I don't know how she stood looking at my brother's things with price tags on them. She desperately wanted my brother's toolbox. My father had pushed off the request a few times but eventually got it. Months later, my father told my sister that emptying the toolbox was one of the most difficult things he had ever done. My mother was upset one day saying she wished they had taken more items, but my father didn't want to. I tried to explain to her that she and my dad were on opposite sides of the same painful fence. She wanted all of Danny's things because it was too painful to let them go. Dad wanted to let them go because it was too painful to have them at the house. Grief is such a self-centered process.

We were lucky and the landlord found the photos we wanted as well as the wallet and the birth certificate. They are where they belong, with my parents.

*   *   *

With this agonizing chapter behind us, we made plans for Easter. When Danny died, I told my sister I knew Easter would be the hardest. We did not usually gather together at other holidays. Everyone would eventually see each other, but in-laws and work schedules made it difficult for everyone to be together at the same time. Easter was different though. Attending the breakfast and the "Big Money Egg Hunt" was a priority. We did gather this Easter. We held the egg hunt, but I couldn't do it. I took pictures as the kids ran around the yard.

My mother turned 70 in April. We held a small family dinner and then invited neighbors to join us for cake. Mom was surprised and seemed to have fun. As we sang Happy Birthday to her, I tried to take a photo with her and the six grandchildren as I had done with my dad at his party that day at Danny's in June. I don't know who was more difficult for the picture, my 11-month-old nephew or his grandmother. My sister stood off to my side trying to get Sam to smile. In each picture, my mother's eyes were focused on my sister instead of smiling at the camera. I eventually asked Martha to stand behind me so ALL the people would know where to look.

*   *   *

In April, my friend's son had a terrible fall and suffered many injuries. She was traveling a great deal to see him so we mostly communicated by email. I started including encouraging Bible verses at the end of my notes. Mary had done it for me so many times and it often made the difference. I found, as I searched books and websites for quotes on healing or encouragement, for every one I found for my friend, I saw 10 that were meaningful to me. Interesting, the more I worked to help someone else with peace and strength, the more I found them for myself.

*   *   *

As Mother's Day approached, I was feeling anxious on all fronts. How would my mother do? Would Diane be expecting me to acknowledge her? Ray was in the area for guard duty and Diane would be coming down to get him when it was over. It would be the night before Mother's Day. He asked if I would get together with them. I had to work in the morning, and then I was walking in a charity 5K. Kate had a game. Allison had a game. Cole had a game and we had church. It was a really full day. Diane had planned to pick Ray up at 4 p.m. but offered to be available earlier as well. I apologized saying the day was already so packed I wouldn't be able to make it. Around seven that night, I saw Ray had left a message on my cell phone. I called him back thinking he was already home. I was surprised when he said the convoy was just pulling back into base. They were behind schedule and he would call me back in a few minutes. When I hung up, I looked at Murph. I told him Ray and Diane were still in the area. My busy day was over; I no longer had a reason (notice I did not say excuse) not to meet. I got in my car and headed north. By the time Ray called back, I was halfway to the base. I asked if they wanted to meet for dinner. Of course, I had some trepidation that Diane would interpret our time together as a "Mother's Day Dinner." On the cruise, one of the professional photographs had been of Ray's daughter with Allison, Cole and Katie at dinner. I purchased it with the intention of giving it to Diane as a thank-you for the cruise. Three months after the trip, I still had it in my possession. I brought it with me. We met for dinner, and for better or worse, the service was exceptionally slow. We had *a lot* of time to chat. I handed Diane a bag with the photo. She seemed happy with it. I have to say, I am always impressed by her composure, no tears or gushing. Ray filled us in on his three-week training; Diane talked about planting a garden. I did not say much. There were only two mentions of Mother's Day. Once when Diane asked if the kids would be serving me breakfast in bed, and once when the waitress wished us a Happy Mother's Day.

On the drive home, I realized I could let go of my worry about Mother's Day. I could not control Diane's thoughts and feelings. If she wanted to interpret the dinner and photo as Mother's Day gifts, I had to let that be. I emailed Mary when I got home. I had talked with her earlier in the day and told her I felt okay about my decision not to meet Ray and Diane. She sounded a tad disappointed. I knew she understood I was busy, but I think she still holds out for that Hallmark moment. That moment where everything is okay and everyone is happy. I wrote her telling how it came to be that I had dinner with Ray and Diane. In the end, I told Mary I did not go for anyone other than myself, but I was sure she would be happy too.

I brought Chinese food to my mom on Mother's Day, her favorite, chicken chow mien. I wanted to give her a gift but she never wants anything, and she rarely needs anything she hasn't already bought for herself. I decided to make her something. I wrote a sequel to my second grade essay. I titled it "My Mother Is Terrific Because . . . Part II." I went on to write she was terrific because she is a great example to me; she is a wonderful grandmother and with her help, I have been able to achieve a balance between work and family. I told her she was terrific because she saved things, things such as my first communion dress. Allison wore the dress 22 years after me and Kate wore it five years after Allison. It was special to see *my* girls in that dress. I was not prepared for the emotion I felt when others gushed about me still having it. The dress did look a little different on each of us. Kate must have been taller than Allison and me at the age of eight. The dress barely came down to Kate's knees and I had to caution her about bending over, no need to show her underwear to *everyone*. Thanks Mom for saving my dress. Mom did not read my essay when I gave it to her; she said she had already cried once that day, and she did not want to do it again.

*   *   *

Life really did start to settle down as summer approached. I felt like the medication was making a difference in my life. I was more even tempered, laughed more often and cried way less. I felt it was the right decision at the right time. Truth be told, it probably would have been the right decision anytime in the past 10 years or so.

We did our normal routine of baseball and softball with the kids. Ray was in the area for guard duty and came to one of Allison's games. He met my father-in-law that day. Diane emailed one night to say she would be passing through my town the next day. She asked if we could meet for lunch. I was working, but if she could be near the mall by my house at 12:30, I could do it. We spent about 45 minutes together and it seemed better. The first few minutes are always tense for me, but it is an improvement as it used to be the first 30 to 40 minutes. While at lunch, Diane told me we were welcome to attend the third of July fireworks as we had done last year. A few days later Richard called to let me know he would be making the trip to his hometown and would be happy to see us there. I drove up with just the kids since Murph could not get out of work early that day. We arrived just before Ray and Richard. I met Diane's fiancé for the first time. We ate dinner and went to the town park for fireworks. It was only one short year earlier when we were meeting Richard for the first time. This year I sat at the table after dinner helping Allison casually braid a friendship bracelet she was making. I took a few opportunities to pick on Ray and Richard. I embraced each of them before we left and I did not feel like I was going to pass out, throw up or disintegrate. How things have changed.

Recently, in church, the deacon's sermon dealt with sowing seeds of the future. He encouraged us, saying you never know when something you have done will cause positive things in another person's life. When we came home, I felt compelled to search through a box for my first letter from

Diane. Almost 16 years ago, she sent a card and the front said, "Tomorrow's dreams will blossom from the seeds we sow today." Talk about a full circle moment.

Ray and I met for lunch recently. He asked if I still feel I made the right decision in meeting everyone. I said yes. Diane emailed me when she first fell in love with the man who is now her fiancé. I wrote back, "Everyone deserves happiness in life. Good for you." They are getting married in September and we are planning to attend. I am nervous about meeting so many people at one time, but Ray said it would be okay for me to wear a sign that says, "Yes, I'm her. Please move along."

I used to live my life according to right or wrong, all or nothing. It was black or white, no shades of gray. I can now see how that developed over the years. These days I know there is a better way to look at the world. I can honestly look back and know I was not *wrong* for refusing to meet Diane 16 years ago; I just wasn't *ready*. It was so much more than not being ready to meet her. I was not ready to face the feelings of hurt and anger. I think Diane, Ray, Richard and I all agree the timing of our meeting worked out for the best. Had I decided to meet them all those years ago, perhaps I would have only met one time and been done. However, I am the first to say, "No what-ifs."

To quote Jenny, "It's not good. It's not bad. It is what it is." Why didn't I pay closer attention the first time she said it so many months ago? I have lightheartedly offered many times over the months to get the saying tattooed on my forearm so I can read it everyday.

I once made the comment to Diane that even unintentional pain hurts. I realize now it is a two way street. I had hurt people too; sometimes on purpose but more times than not, I didn't mean to do it. I am reminded of Danny's words to me last April, "I wasn't trying to hurt anyone; I just had problems." *I am right there with ya brother.*

Epilogue

The unexpected journey led me to peace and understanding. It also led me to Grand Cayman and Mexico. The biggest roadblock along the way was my own thinking. One book I recently read stated that only the brave face their pain. Not to pat myself on the back, but I believe it to be entirely true. I had to put myself out on a limb, a really fragile limb, examining my thoughts, actions and beliefs. I was lucky to have people in my life that literally held the branch up so it did not break. Some supported me and others challenged me, but they all have my respect and admiration.

I almost titled this book *Finding My Missing Piece*. I wasn't sure if I would spell it piece or peace; either would have worked. Once I started to let that wall come down, I was able to see how I had closed myself off from so much and more importantly, so many. The piece that had been missing was an understanding of my true self. Once I could admit to who I really was, a good person with some flaws, I did find an unbelievable peace. My brother is gone. Some might say there is nothing I can do about that now, but I don't think it is true. I believe there is a lot that I can still do. I can keep his memory alive by continuing to share our adventures with my children and hopefully, his children too. I can emulate his open and forgiving attitude as I move forward in my own life. Lastly, I can learn how to make clams casino, although unlike Danny, I will leave out the green peppers.

*   *   *

Along this journey, people have asked me my thoughts on open adoption. I am supportive of it as an option. Both the birth family and the adoptive family need to agree though. I don't think it is a concept that can work if both sides are not fully committed to staying in touch. I also don't think you can live a number of years with a closed adoption and easily transition to an open one. This book is about my story, it is not meant to advise anyone about search or reunion. If someone were to ask me how to go about connecting, I would strongly advocate the use of a third party person like a confidential intermediary, a lawyer or a friend. Time, space and patience are critical.

*   *   *

Many times in my life, I swore I would never again take things or people for granted. I made this pledge after September 11, again after the death of my mother-in-law and again after my lumpectomy. After the death of my brother, I try to remind myself of this pledge daily. Perhaps that was my problem in the past, I would vow to live life to the fullest, to act like each day might be my last, and then, I would forget.

I no longer take my relationship with God for granted either (or at least I try not to). Several times in these pages, I talk about feeling *compelled* to act. I was not always sure why I had certain thoughts or who convinced me to take particular actions. I am now confident that God indeed watches me and when I need Him, His hand gently guides me.

I know a family who lost their 12-year-old son after a heart transplant. The parents performed the entire funeral service themselves. I was in awe of their faith, strength and courage. The father spoke of when the son was born with multiple heart defects. As he looked at his infant son, he heard a voice say, "God's timing is perfect." Twelve years later, as the son was gravely ill, the father said he heard the voice tell him once again, "God's timing is perfect."

I have come to understand that not everything that happens in my life is on *my* timeline. Perhaps the reason something did or didn't happen was that the timing was not right for someone else. This unexpected journey has been hard and painful at times but the rewards have been numerous and beautiful. I hope this is a feeling that stays with me for the rest of my life.